THRIVE

THRIVE

Channel Your Courage, Speak Your Truth,
and SHINE in the Midst of Life's Challenges

Donna Clark Love
Erin Jones
Jenny Severson, EdD
Mary Smith
Tami West, PhD

ISBN: 978-0-578-64211-6

Cover design and butterfly illustration created and copyrighted (2020) by Carrie Carlson.

Page layout by Win-Win Words LLC.

Printed in the United States of America.

We dedicate this book to you. Our stories are your stories. You are stronger than you think, more courageous than you realize, and more precious than the finest rubies. Share your heart with others—even if it has been broken. Raise your voice on behalf of those who have no voice. Stay open to possibilities. Give yourself permission to thrive with grit, passion and humor. Create new chapters for your life. Change your world. It is time to shine!

CONTENTS

INTRODUCTION

W E ARE THE **SPEAKER SISTERS**, A SMALL band of five women from different walks of life, embracing the challenge of moving beyond surviving every day to thriving. In this book we weave together techniques, anecdotes, and the magic of storytelling to guide you through life's uncertain and difficult times. Our goal is to help you discover blessings within difficulties. It is not just about getting through life changes; it's also about using them as a launching pad for joy.

As former educators and now educational consultants, we are passionate about supporting one another. We are equally passionate about supporting all women in the workplace. We understand the challenges you face every day in the classroom and in your lives as women, mothers, sisters, wives, caregivers, and colleagues.

This book is dedicated to you! You have chosen a profession where you are expected to wear many hats. Not only are you expected to be a content expert, you are expected to be data collector, test giver, therapist, motivator, detective, YouTube entertainer, mediator, surrogate parent, wellness coordinator, stand-up comic, decorator, dietician, miracle worker, and too many other titles to list.

Do any of the following statements resonate with you?

Why can't I get along with people who have different (or difficult) personalities?

Why can't I be "normal" like everyone else and stop worrying?

What will happen to me if/when . . . ?

I feel like a fraud; I'm a horrible teacher; I'm just not good enough.

I'm tired of coping with my workload by using food, alcohol, prescription drugs, sex, narcotics, or whatever my drug of choice might be.

Why can't I take care of myself? Why do I put everyone else's needs before mine?

Why is the bully targeting me?

Will I ever recover from this trauma?

How can I adequately meet the needs of my family and my own children in the midst of all my work responsibilities?

Why can't I be more grateful for what I do have?

Are these thoughts getting in the way of your becoming the person you want to be, both inside and outside the classroom? Your education career might last one year or it might last thirty-five years (or more). Too many women are struggling to survive day to day. How much better would it be to thrive not only professionally but also personally!

No other book out there will impact your lives as this one will! Each chapter is filled with our personal stories of falling down and getting back up—of overcoming and soaring. We have made every effort throughout the book to be transparent about our own struggles. You will read about humor coexisting with heartbreak. We will also share our essential moments of grace, such as:

- Tami opening up about her lifetime battle with mental illness, to include her stay in a psychiatric hospital after student teaching.

- Mary discussing how going through a divorce while teaching impacted her and consequently led to her subjecting a student to the worst year of his academic career.
- Donna painstakingly revealing how food addiction and her negative body image nearly destroyed her life.
- Jenny sharing what she learned during the hardest year of her life, including her battle with cancer.
- Erin relating her journey from being abandoned by her biological mother as a baby and years later losing a major statewide election to finding God's excellent plan for her life.

We will share life lessons with you, based on our own experiences, actual events, and proven research. You will laugh, cry, shake your head in disbelief, be challenged and inspired, and, at times, *drop your jaw in awe!*

Your life is about to change! We believe that you can become a person of action, overcome any obstacle, and scale any height. Work through the book alone or with other teachers. Write on the pages. Dog-ear the sections that speak to you most profoundly. Journal after each chapter. Be intentional about the tips you will implement. A marvelous professional and personal life awaits you. THRIVE *is a must-read for those women who want to live a 'great-full,' authentic, purposeful, fully present, grace-filled, fulfilling life.*

THRIVE

Meet Donna Clark Love

Donna Clark Love is an internationally recognized bully expert, workshop trainer, and conference keynote speaker. She is a licensed counselor for the chemically dependent, a certified trainer for Stephen Covey's "Seven Habits of Highly Effective People," and a certified mediator/conflict resolution trainer. Donna has been featured on NBC's *Today* show and the *NBC Evening News* to highlight successful prevention programming.  She has been featured in *Forbes* magazine on workplace bullying. She has also been asked to provide expert commentary on digital bullying/harassment for *Good Morning America.* In 2005, *People* magazine recognized her as the "cyber bullying expert."

In October 2003, she was asked to highlight effective bullying prevention policies for the National Department of Education. Donna has trained on Indian reservations, U.S. Air Force bases, and worked with the Maori Tribe in New Zealand. Contracted by the Belizean government, she trained government employees and teachers on how to combat bullying and workplace violence. In February 2018, Donna trained and consulted with NASA/Johnson Space Center employees on addressing culture, peer conflicts, and digital bullying via social media. She especially values her work with nonprofit organizations, principally churches, and she has preached sermons and conducted workshops for her local church, Mercy Street.

The success of Donna's groundbreaking and dynamic trainings has gained her international recognition. She was asked to speak at the June 2018 International Workplace Bullying and Harassment Conference in Bordeaux, France. Donna is a captivating speaker who connects, empathizes, engages, and inspires her audiences to make lasting changes.

Meet Donna Clark Love

Follow Donna Clark Love
Consultant/Trainer/Speaker
281/467-4861
Donna@Clark-Love.com
www.bullyingexpert.com
@bullyexpert1

1

BEFORE YOU TAKE THAT FIRST BITE . . . READ THIS

Donna Clark Love

"You are altogether beautiful,
my darling; there is no flaw in you."
Song of Songs 4:7

WHAT IF YOU COULD EMBRACE A WORLD where people could admit their struggles . . . and come clean about the secrets that isolate and cloud your vision of who you truly are?

One of my greatest struggles as a woman, an educator, a churchgoer, a family member, and a friend has been to admit that I am a compulsive overeater, a food addict, and a ruthless critic when it comes to my weight. Let me tell you a secret: Pre-recovery, if you and I dined together and there was a basketful of chips sitting between us, I could not focus on what you were saying. I would try, but, really, I was focused on not consuming the entire basket. After we said our good-byes, even if I had eaten a hearty dinner, I would hit my favorite haunts, the drive-thrus that happened to be open late. Satiated with french fries, cheese enchiladas, cheeseburgers, and day-old doughnuts, feeling sick and numb, I would still trudge home to ravish what was left in my cupboards.

"My name is Donna and I am a food addict who is powerless over refined sugar and things made with white flour."

What other term would you use for a woman who gets into her car at 11:30 at night, in a dangerous snowstorm, and drives six miles to the 7-Eleven to get sour cream and onion potato chips, Little Debbies, and a bag full of chocolate candy? Even though she is gaining weight, and feeling profoundly guilty and shameful after each nightly binge, and though she resolves to stop this behavior, she does it almost every night, night after night.

This is food addiction.

I am not talking about the kind of overindulgence that has become a celebrated part of American culture, like overeating on Thanksgiving. I am not talking about "normies" who leave uneaten dessert on their plates, who gain a little weight and decide to cut down. No. I am talking about those of us for whom the idea of food isn't one of pleasure, but of compulsion. Those of us whose thoughts of food, and the effects of food, are the constant, dreary background static to normal thoughts. Those of us who walk into the school lounge packed with desserts in a state of panic and breathlessly eat slice after slice of banana bread—not even tasting it—until the panic can be drowned in a meditative routine of chewing and swallowing, chewing and swallowing.

Don't stop reading just because you have not struggled as I have. This chapter will be of help to anyone who might be caught in your own vicious cycle of judging yourself harshly concerning your relationship with food, your weight, or even your body perception.

My eating career started at thirteen. I found that I could stuff my feelings, anxieties, and fears about boys with extra food. It was as if I could not get enough of anything and that feeling of being full was unattainable. The summer before my eighth-grade year, I gained forty pounds. In the many years that followed, I lost and gained hundreds of pounds.

For most of my adult life, I was extremely overweight. I was an overachiever, an excellent student, the 'most fun to be with senior' in my high school, the president of my junior and senior classes at my university, a Bible study teacher, a beloved educator and mentor . . . *yet, the one thing I could not do was stop overeating.* In my mind, this one thing negated all the good in my life. I felt ashamed of my size, and saw myself as a hypocrite for spouting about God's love and mercy when I felt unworthy, unlovable, and hopeless.

I hit bottom after my first year of teaching. I could no longer face another student and pretend all was well. My insides had caught up with my outsides. I resigned my position as a debate coach and that summer sought help at a pastoral counseling center, where I was introduced to a twelve-step program that eventually changed my life. At this center, for the first time in many years, I felt accepted and loved even with the extra weight on my body. I found it was not about what I was eating, *it was about what was eating me.* I also discovered I needed help. I needed counseling, support, and large quantities of self-forgiveness. This experience set me on a journey for which I will be forever grateful. I began to work a twelve-step program that taught me a framework for living one day at a time and helped me to find a way of eating that was not a diet but a way of life. For the last thirty-four years, I have been involved in twelve-step recovery and have maintained an overall 100-pound weight loss for more than twenty of those years.

Despite our culture's obsession with food, weight loss, and body size, we are still uncomfortable placing food in the context of addiction. People compulsively overeat for the same reasons they take drugs, but we are quicker to understand the idea of someone being a drug addict.

In recent years, food addiction has become a popular subject among some scientists. Many researchers agree that certain foods high in fat, sugar, and salt are addictive and cause changes in the brain similar to those produced by drugs. Studies in animals have shown that rats that binge on sugar can develop signs of dependency. Although there is little doubt that eating can stimulate the release of feel-good chemicals in the brain, there is evidence that it's the behavior—the restrict/binge cycle—that can cause the signs of dependency.

For some researchers, the idea of food addiction is controversial. Some researchers have even stated that the term "eating addiction" is a more accurate term than "food addiction." It is not my intent to debate specific research findings, terminology, the etymology of eating disorders, and/or comment on whether food addiction is or is not a disease. All I know and what is true for me aligns with the following study conducted by NEDA (National Eating Disorders Association): "Recent research has determined that binge eaters' brains surge with dopamine at the sight and smell of certain trigger foods, in the same way that cocaine addicts' brains respond to lines on a mirror."

However, one does not have to possess an eating disorder or food addiction to struggle with body image. As Brené Brown PhD discovered in her research on women and shame, nearly all women feel ashamed of their bodies at one time or another. Combined research studies claim that 90 percent of women in our society, if asked the question, "Are you satisfied/happy with your current weight?" emphatically answer "No!" Based on DSM-IV criteria, by age six, girls start to express concerns about their own weight or shape. Between 40-60 percent of elementary school girls (ages six to twelve) are concerned about their weight or about becoming too fat. This concern endures through life. Some of us carry around a lifetime of shame due to our inability to measure up to culturally defined standards of perfection.

Women's judgment and/or hatred of their bodies is such a common phenomenon that we pay no heed to how deeply it undercuts our sense of self-worth, saps our mental and emotional energy, and ultimately undermines our personal and collective power. It's the teenage girl who doesn't know she's beautiful; it's the woman in her twenties who doesn't understand that "men like a woman with curves"; it's the middle-aged woman frowning in front of the mirror as she realizes that menopause has resulted in the shifting of weight on her previously thin frame; it's the woman who just had twins and is exercising frantically trying to get back to her pre-baby weight. It's the thirty-five-year-old who thinks if she could lose five more pounds, she could be happy. It's the elderly woman, reaching the end of her life, still engaged in the yo-yo dieting in an attempt to look presentable before she dies.

In *How to Be a Woman*, Caitlin Moran encourages women to see themselves as "human-shaped."[1] What if we reframed the often-quoted phrase, "Inside every fat woman there is a thin woman trying to get out." I actually would like the quote to be changed to, "Inside every female, there's a human being trying to be noticed, heard, and accepted for who she is right now!"

Some of us are still plagued by childhood teasing and bullying about our bodies. We carry these memories in our DNA. I still recall vividly when a high school friend of mine asked a cute boy I had a crush on if he would go to the Christmas Coronation Dance with me. His response: "Donna is so fat. I never date fat girls."

There is a scene in the 1989 film *Shirley Valentine* where Shirley expresses shock at her lover, Costas, daring to kiss her stretch marks:

Shirley: "You kissed my stretch marks!"

Costas: "Don't try to hide these lines. They are lovely,

because they are part of you, and you are lovely, so don't hide . . . be proud. These marks show that you are alive and that you survived. They are the marks of your life. Cherish them."

I get frustrated with myself because every once in a while, I will hyper-focus on the perfect bodies in magazines and on billboards that most likely have been digitally enhanced. Why does the fashion industry still make the cutest clothes for six-foot-tall, flat androgynes? Some of us believe that no matter how much weight we lose, it will never be enough. Should we just throw in the towel now? Is our only alternative to embark on a lifetime of miserable attempts at self-improvement, judging ourselves unmercifully for every pound we gain or lose? Maybe there are some things we can do to alter this way of thinking and living.

I had a rude awakening when even after losing the excess pounds and being at a normal weight, I was *not* enormously happy. All my dreams did *not* come true just because the extra pounds were gone. Had my weight or my perception of my body size served as a smokescreen to keep me from taking risks, following my dreams, and walking through my fears?

I found over a period of time judging myself about my weight—good or bad—was not the answer to my happiness. I have been a large-size model and a small-size model. Whether on a runway, or in a photo shoot . . . *what matters is not my body size* . . . what matters is how I feel about myself at that exact moment. The self-improvement I desired was an inside job, and it had very little to do with the scale. I had to begin to address my perceptions and judgments about my body size. I had to look at the signs, symptoms, and causes that got me to eat my way up the scale. I had to find a way to end this tug-of-war with my body and my distorted perceptions. I had to discover how to live life without using the buffer of sugar and extra carbs. I had to develop new tools for feeling all my feelings, even the uncomfortable ones.

Today, I am not that woman obsessed with the thought of food, consumed with thinking about when I will be able to sneak away and numb out my feelings with another binge. I am not focused 24/7 on how "thin" or "fat" or "perfect" my body is according to my sometimes-critical standards or society's. I do not have all the answers, but I am willing to learn and grow. I am focused on progress . . .not perfection. There are days I still wake up and see a 240-pound woman in the mirror; the difference is that now I have hope and a path of recovery to help me when those distortions arise. I have tools I can use to shift my focus to what's going on inside me, not what I see in the mirror.

So far, I have been talking about my own experiences with compulsive overeating, body shame and having a distorted body image. Maybe you can relate to someone who is putting their life on hold and living in the 'if only' phrases. Phrases that sound like this: "If only I could lose these extra 2, 3, 5, 10, 20, and so on pounds . . . Then I could start dating, truly be more content, wear cuter clothes, participate in a marathon, be more attractive, go on a trip, etc."

Following are some strategies you can utilize or share if you or someone you know is struggling with body shame, food issues, and/or distorted body perceptions:

- Check out negative or distorted thinking about your appearance and/or body size with someone else who will tell you the truth.

- Practice accepting your body no matter how much you weigh.

- Take a shower and dress becomingly, even when your body shame is overpowering.

- Do one thing you have been putting off until you lose (fill in the blank) pounds.
- Stop punishing yourself.
- Write a gratitude list for the parts of your body that you can be grateful for.
- Abstain from perusing fashion magazines that promote perfection.
- Let go of perfection.
- Compliment and affirm other women.
- Bask in God's loving presence.

Being a compulsive overeater/food addict without hope and a solution can be compared to the crack addict who does not know where the next fix will come from. You might not personally suffer as a food addict, but I bet you come in contact with students and staff members who suffer with an eating disorder. Your awareness of eating addictions can equip you to offer support in aiding someone struggling to break the shame of this compulsive cycle. Awareness is the first step toward recovery for those who need help and for those who are willing to offer support.

Myths and misconceptions surround eating addictions, and these can make it more difficult for you to provide effective help to your students, friends, or family members who might be struggling with these issues. The National Eating Disorders Association (NEDA) created a series of tool kits for parents, educators, and coaches to help dispel myths and provide accurate, up-to-date information in an easy-to-use guidebook. Some of the questions and issues that you will see addressed in the tool kit are:

- What are eating disorders?

- What are some signs that one of my students or staff members might have an eating disorder?
- What is the overall impact of eating disorders on cognitive ability and functioning, and how specifically do they affect student academic performance?
- What school resources and outside organizations can I recommend for help?

First and foremost, if you are a compulsive overeater and truly struggle with a food addiction, I suggest that you connect to a support system such as OA or HOW (twelve-step programs for overeaters). Overeaters Anonymous (OA) offers a program of recovery from compulsive overeating, binge eating, and other eating disorders. OA is not just about weight loss, weight gain, or diets. It addresses physical, emotional, and spiritual well-being.

There are also other avenues of support, including church recovery programs, online support and blogging platforms, therapeutic groups with trained professionals, nutritionists, wellness coaches, and so on.

Since NEDA has provided educators with a comprehensive tool kit complete with current research-based strategies and tools, I would like to also provide you with the some of the top strategies from my LOVE tool kit that has worked for my life and the lives of many other women. (You can download the complete LOVE tool kit at www.bullyingexpert.com) Whether you are an occasional emotional eater, a holiday overeater, a chocoholic, a salt junkie, a woman who has gained weight due to menopause, someone who would just like to shed a few pounds, someone who undereats when stressed, or someone who binges, purges, compulsively overeats, and/or has been diagnosed with an eating disorder . . . this tool kit might be of help to you.

Some effective tips from the LOVE tool kit are as follows:

- Learn what triggers emotional eating.

- Make a list of things to do when you get the urge to eat and you're not hungry, and always carry it with you.

- When the overwhelming desire arises to use food to check out, numb a painful feeling, distract from doing a difficult task, or simply to relieve boredom, try one or more of these non-food-related activities:

  o Get moving.

  o If at school, go talk to another fellow teacher and ask questions about him/her.

  o Listen to your favorite music.

  o Read something you enjoy for twenty minutes.

  o Take ten slow, deep breaths.

  o Write in a journal, color, draw, or blog about your feelings.

  o Go to a twelve-step meeting or any other support framework where you feel accepted.

  o Get on your knees and pray, pray, pray.

  o Call someone who also struggles with food addiction.

  o Make an appointment with a therapist, sponsor, or life coach.

  o Watch a Netflix movie. (Notice I did not say binge-watch a Netflix series.)

  o Practice mindfulness exercises.

- Make regular meals a habit. It has worked for me to have a measured and balanced food plan. Skipping meals sets me up to be overly hungry, and then I would choose foods high in fat and sugar . . . *which eventually led to a binge.*

- Eat breakfast every day. Little did I realize that by eating breakfast daily, my mid-morning hunger could be curbed.
- Maintain an attitude of gratitude by making a gratitude list daily.
- Stay in your day; you can do mostly anything one day at a time.

Part of my journey of healing has been and continues to be telling my story. It is important for people to know that food addiction can affect anyone. The obsession can steal your joy, rob you of your dreams, and leave you feeling defeated and hopeless. I believe that my ministry is to encourage fellow sufferers and carry the message that there is hope, healing, and restoration available to anyone who reaches for it.

I have learned to face each day with an awareness and acceptance that this will be a lifelong process. My food addiction can be arrested if I am willing to do what it takes to recover. Most days, I have freedom from the desire and/or obsession to overeat and/or partake of sugary substances and items made with white flour. I did not even take a bite of my cake at my wedding. I now eat to live, not live to eat. This is a true miracle.

God has granted me the grace and willingness to go to whatever lengths it takes to maintain my peace, my sane way of eating, and my healthier body image. Through a lot of hard work, reflection, prayer, and support, on more days than not, I have also come to accept my body size and weight. I have come a long way from having nine different sizes of clothing in my closet due to the erratic dieting and overeating I did for so many years! It is so wonderful to wear the same size of clothing year after year. But even more wonderful is being relieved of the food obsession and the gnawing need to weigh and link my self-esteem to the number on the scale.

There are solutions! There are avenues of help for you! All you have to do is reach out, admit you have a problem, and then ask for help.

My Challenge to You:

Set aside time to think about your relationship with food. Do you relate to any of the behaviors outlined in this chapter, such as: Eating more food or sugar when you're feeling bored, anxious, overwhelmed, fearful, or lonely? Eating less when you're stressed out? Do you have or have you ever had an eating disorder?

If so, consider what actions you might need/want to take to create a healthier relationship with food. Many tools and avenues of support have been listed in this chapter—which ones may be a place for you to start making positive changes?

Journal Prompts:

Write about how you feel about your body. Do you recognize yourself in any of the many descriptions of women listed in this chapter? If so, write about what you related to—the parts that made you go, "That's *me*!"

Are you uncomfortable with your size or certain parts of your body? If so, write down some kind and loving statements about those parts of your body (the kinds of things you would say to a friend who was criticizing her body).

2
BULLYING IN THE SCHOOLHOUSE: ADULTS ONLY!

Donna Clark Love

"Therefore, as God's chosen people, holy and dearly loved, clothe yourselves with compassion, kindness, humility, gentleness, and patience. Bear with each other and forgive one another if any of you has a grievance against someone. Forgive as the Lord forgave you. And over all these virtues put on love, which binds them all together in perfect unity."
Colossians 3:12-14

WHAT IF WE WORKED IN AN ATMOSPHERE where kindness prevailed, where all opinions were welcomed, where respectful behaviors were the norm? What if we agreed to disagree? What if we looked forward to working together in our team meetings? What if we enjoyed engaging in faculty meetings? What if we trusted our leaders to do the right thing when adult bullying was being exhibited?

After teaching for twenty years, I was recruited for a position that changed the trajectory of my career. The job description was a dream come true because my job responsibilities matched my natural skills and talents. As I signed all my papers, I did not realize that I was walking into a world where I would be micromanaged, belittled, bullied, betrayed, and at times tormented.

15

Within three months of receiving this new position, I was walking on eggshells, internalizing the criticism, and becoming hyper-vigilant about every move I made. I was scapegoated for my supervisor's mishaps and lack of knowledge about certain initiatives. I felt anxious, less-than, and lived in constant fear. My work was stolen, and the authorship of many documents I created was changed from my name to my supervisor's name. When the press came to film my department's special projects and highlights, I was asked to re-route the press to my supervisor's office to film— with her as the narrator. I was not included. My supervisor would become irrational and would yell or berate me behind closed doors. The more successful and recognized I became for the excellent programs my department was facilitating . . . the more the bullying escalated.

Some of you might relate to the actual events in my story; some of you might relate to the feelings. Some of you might only think about bullying in reference to particular students in your school because this is typically the only framework in which bullying is discussed.

Student bullies come in all shapes and sizes. There's Paige, an eight-year-old, who uses her physical size and toughness to intimidate her classmates. Jermaine, a lanky eighth grader, gets what he wants in more subtle ways; his quick wit and caustic comments cause his classmates to comply with his wishes. Mary, the prom queen and captain of the soccer team, controls who is allowed in her coveted exclusive social circle and who can only watch from the sidelines. Without intervention, the majority of these children will likely become adults who perpetuate these behaviors beyond the schoolhouse.

Although the ways in which these students bully others differ, the results are the same. They coerce, marginalize, and dominate. Just knowing the possibility that these bullies could behave this way is enough to create an atmosphere of terror. Every school has bullies. However, we can minimize their influence and sometimes actually stop the bullying by establishing reporting procedures and creating action plans with expectations, setting the tone, monitoring behaviors, and enforcing consequences.

Bullying isn't limited to children. There are adult bullies in our schools, too. Mr. Holmes, a lead teacher, is a bully. He can be very sarcastic and frightening in comments to his students, but the most profound ways he bullies is with his colleagues. Mr. Holmes has very fixed views on education; any deviation from his expectations is met with a malicious comment, a harsh glance, ridicule, and, in some cases, a full-blown character assassination. Because he has no reservations about the toll his cruel remarks might make on others, and because he has not received any kind of admonishment or consequence for his actions—and because others are aware of this—Mr. Holmes is given reign over the campus, and he has an unwarranted amount of influence. It's not that other faculty members respect his judgment; rather, it's that his colleagues want to avoid a confrontation and escape his scorn.

Every school has a Mr. Holmes, usually more than one. There is also the extremely skilled, popular, and 'recognized' teacher, Mrs. Hernandez, who wields her influence through her finely honed social skills. Mrs. Hernandez can be the 'sniper' who will praise you to your face and then, when you turn your back, all hell breaks loose. Whether she intimidates, gossips, excludes or humiliates others, her behavior is ignored or tacitly accepted by others. As a faculty, we dismiss what she does and make excuses: "That's just the way

Mrs. Hernandez is," or we might say, "Mrs. Hernandez is the best teacher we have; she must be having a bad day."

Why do we do this? We discipline students who try to intimidate, control, or take advantage of others, so why do we allow adults to get away with this behavior?

Too often, we limit our focus to teachers' interactions with their students. We wouldn't tolerate an acerbic response to a student, but we ignore the sarcastic comment to a colleague.

Bullying is frighteningly more common in the workplace than one might assume. A cumulative study by the University of Sheffield, Harvard, USC, the RAND Corp, & the Workplace Bullying Institute (WBI) has shown that approximately three out of every ten people have experienced bullying at the workplace in the last six months. The research discovered that 14-20 percent of people felt they were a victim of cyber bullying at least once a week. In 2013, WBI completed a survey among organizations and employees from a variety of careers and found that two of the top professions where bullying is most prevalent are among nurses and teachers.

Workplace bullying can cause anxiety, stress, and hostility, eventually leading to declines in employee productivity, negative effects on overall climate, and, sometimes, the resignations of the best employees. We have lost some great educators over the years! It is important for all of us to recognize and take action against bullying in order to maintain sustainable business operations, as well as successful schools.

While there is no magic wand to completely prevent or end bullying, there are a few promising strategies that can be used to combat bullying and improve culture. Many experts agree that addressing the culture is the key to bullying/harassment prevention. This begins with the awareness of 'what is' and 'what is not' considered true bullying behaviors.

What Is Workplace Bullying?

School bullying is often clearly defined by policy, legislation, and law. This is often not the case with workplace bullying. It's difficult to specifically define workplace bullying, unless the behavior is part of other legislatively protected areas such as harassment, discrimination, or intimidation. Researchers and experts agree that bullying usually involves repeated incidents or a pattern of behavior intended to intimidate, offend, degrade, or humiliate a particular person or group. In the simplest of terms, bullying can be defined as persistent and ongoing acts of incivility directed toward an individual or group. This definition works for both workplace and student-to-student bullying.

What are examples of bullying?

Often, workplace bullying targets don't even recognize threatening and intimidating behavior as bullying until someone specifically identifies it. The following list is not a comprehensive checklist of all bullying behaviors, but it offers some specific examples to be aware of.

Examples include:

- Spreading malicious rumors, gossip, personal history, or innuendo.

- Admonishing, excluding, or isolating someone in team meetings, faculty meetings, group events, and social gatherings.

- Intimidating, making fun of, or threatening a person in front of students, parents, or other staff members.

- Undermining or deliberately impeding a person's work.

- Establishing impossible deadlines that will set an individual up to fail.

- Withholding necessary information or purposefully giving the wrong information; removing areas of responsibilities without cause.

- Making jokes that are 'obviously offensive' verbally or electronically.

- Intruding on a person's privacy by pestering, spying, or stalking.

- Assigning unreasonable duties or workloads unfavorable to one person (in a way that creates unnecessary pressure or harm).

- Yelling, using profanity.

- Criticizing a person persistently; belittling a person's opinions. Sarcasm, rolled eyes, and loud sighs or offensive gestures when someone is talking.

- Blocking requests or applications for training, leave, or staff in-services.

- Tampering with a person's personal belongings, classroom supplies, or work equipment. This includes plagiarizing others' lesson plans.

Cyber-bullying is the new face of bullying. It incorporates the use of electronic devices as a medium for communication with the intent to hurt, embarrass, threat, intimidate, humiliate, or harass another person. The rise of online networking and the increased use of social media has increased the risks for cyber-bullying, harassment, and other forms of victimization. It can quickly spill from onscreen to offscreen and affect the face-to-face interactions between educators at work and away from work. Left unchecked or handled inappropriately, it can create serious problems for school organizations, individuals, and teams. Cyber-bullying incidents include, but are not limited to:

- Malicious, belittling, or threatening e-mails, group texts, and tweets.
- Electronic communications that contain jokes about ethnicity, religion, politics, or any topic that makes an individual uncomfortable.
- Public shaming via a mass e-mail, especially targeting one's job performance or teaching style or spreading lies and gossip—via social networking sites.

Five Ways to Begin Addressing School/District Level Bullying:

1. Identify what a bully and a target look like. Bullies are not always easy to spot. Sometimes the signs of bullying are overt, including yelling, threats, coercion, belittlement, and humiliation, which are easy to see. When bullies take a covert approach to tormenting their targets, this slow and insidious treatment can be almost impossible for anyone outside the interpersonal interaction to identify.

Having good skills, or perhaps *the bully being one of the best teachers in the building,* can also protect bullies and even bring them rewards. Paradoxically, bullies' toxic and destructive behaviors are driven by having a bad attitude, but when they look good on evaluations due to great performance reviews, supervisors and principals often overlook their bad attitudes, and these 'talented tyrants' are praised as successful employees. It is imperative that we all recognize the signs of bullying and not let a great skill set skew how we address the employee who is exhibiting bullying behavior.

A significant difference between student bullying and bullying among educators lies in the characteristics of the chosen target. Remember that all bullies, whether students or adults, go shopping for their targets.

Often, student bullies harass others based on a target's lack of social connection, tendency to be a loner, and perceived *weaknesses*. Some examples of perceived weaknesses can include physical size, age difference, learning challenges and/or high performance, lack of involvement in school activities, social status, being the new kid on the block, etc. By contrast, workplace bullies usually choose their targets based on perceived *strengths*. A few examples of perceived strengths include: physical skills, subject matter expertise, popularity, leadership, tenure, rank, astute social skills, and high performance. Sometimes the target is the one who speaks out against injustices.

2. Name it; Claim it; Call it what it is. Choose a name—bullying, mistreatment, psychological harassment, or emotional violence/abuse. There is tremendous healing power in naming the problem because the source is external to ourselves. A person does not invite, nor want, the methodical campaign of psychological assaults and the resulting interference with school or work performance. No sane person wakes up each day hoping to be humiliated or berated at school or work.

3. Establish a detailed definition of 'workplace civility' or 'respectful school behaviors.' Did you know that a lot of employees and school staff typically lack the adequate knowledge of workplace civility, because we say things like, "Speak nicely," or "Be courteous," or "Treat each other with respect," or "Maintain the highest standards of professionalism."? Phrases like these are wide open to interpretation, including very poor interpretations. If you would like to view an outline of specific expectations of what 'workplace civility' looks like, including attitudinal examples, please refer to my website www.bullyingexpert.com.

4. Let it begin with me. Are you willing to take a look in the mirror? As supervisors, team leaders, principals, teachers, parents, school paraprofessionals . . . do you show respect for others' opinions even when you don't agree? Do you allow room for everyone's voices? Do you make cutting comments or disregard those whose views do not match your own? When you get angry with others, do you express your anger in a healthy manner or do you blow up, say things you regret later, or even silently punish individuals by exclusion?

We need to begin by looking at our own behaviors. We might not be the true bullies, but we might be exhibiting hurtful behaviors that fit on the bullying continuum. To address this, assessments need to be completed both individually and as an organization. Refer to sample assessments at www.bullying-expert.com. Standards for faculty conduct, teamwork, and professionalism need to be directly addressed in faculty meetings, communications, and in end-of-year evaluations.

5. Educate and train all stakeholders. There is overwhelming research that supports organizations conducting bullying prevention/intervention trainings. Employees and organizations at all levels benefit from interactive, skill-based training in order to create and maintain workplaces that are respectful and both physically and emotionally safe. For so long now, we have been intentional about training our staff/employees to address bullying among students. It is high time we be intentional about training and addressing bullying among staff and all adults we interact with. We need to be mindful to include all school staff in this: school secretaries, custodians, cafeteria workers, and bus drivers.

I worked in a school once where the principal's secretary was the biggest bully on campus. She controlled the school with her rage, hurtful sarcasm, and perceived power. Bullies can also be found among the parent population. *How many times have we accepted or tolerated abusive interchanges with parents?*

What Can You Do if You Think You Are Being Bullied?

If you feel that you are being bullied, discriminated against, victimized, or subjected to any form of harassment, the following suggestions might be of assistance. These strategies are not comprehensive. I have found that individual schools, school districts, organizations, and businesses usually have their own protocol for reporting and in-house action plans for addressing bullying incidents.

If you refer to the beginning of this chapter, where I shared my own bullying story, you will notice that my story is incomplete. I am now going to detail the action plan I utilized in my situation. After fervent prayer, and while adhering to the research strategies of Dan Olweus, a Norwegian research professor considered the "pioneer" in bullying research, I took the following steps:

1. I kept a journal of daily events. I kept copies of all pertinent letters, memos, e-mails, faxes, etc. I recorded each incident and included:

- The date, time, and what happened in as much detail as possible.
- The names of witnesses.
- The outcome of the event.

2. After writing out three re-occurring incidents, I scheduled a meeting with my immediate supervisor to read the incidents and tell her that her behavior was unacceptable and it needed to stop. This confrontation was met with resistance, and I left her office quickly.

3. I then followed the chain of command and scheduled a meeting with my supervisor and her supervisor. Without expressing a lot of feeling words, I reported the facts and read the incidents. This time I specified expectations. For example,

I shared that, from that day forward, I would not meet with my supervisor alone in a closed-door office, and I would not accept her calls unless there was another person who could listen. I had four other expectations, but when I began to list them, I was interrupted by her supervisor and was told explicitly not to continue. She told me I was being too harsh, too sensitive, and just ridiculous. She reiterated that my supervisor was a lovely Christian woman who would not engage in the type of behaviors I had outlined, and the meeting was called to a stop. I quickly exited the office.

4. Next, I scheduled a meeting with my supervisor's boss, again following the chain of command. I also filed a detailed grievance report to HR. At this point, I was feeling very defeated and unsupported, and I was seriously considering leaving my job mid-year. My emotional, physical, and spiritual health were being compromised.

5. However, before I even met with my supervisor's boss, I received a message to attend an organizational meeting to hear about the new realignment of strategic personnel and the departmental changes that would be implemented in January. My supervisor was beyond shocked when her name was not only removed from the alignment chart, but her *department* was also removed.

6. I was taken out of my supervisor's department, and my department remained intact. I was told to report to another divisional head, and I never had to deal with my bully again.

Not all bullying scenarios end with a positive or acceptable outcome like mine did. If you believe that faculty members learning and growing together is essential to school success, and if you believe that teachers will perform better when they are engaged and feel positive about coming to school, then you have an obligation to make sure they are not subject to bullying from their peers and/or administrators. Just like addressing bullying among students, reducing bullying among faculty members begins with intention and focus, and it needs to be followed up with commitment and action.

All of us need to have conversations about respect being integral to all interactions in a school—student to student, adult to student, and adult to adult—and we need to model respectful behavior. We also need to discuss what *respect* means—to lay a foundation of understanding to build upon. Often the cultural differences in how one shows respect and expects respect to be given are overlooked, which creates systemic problems that continue to go unaddressed.

The example needs to be set by the adult staff in our school systems. A teacher, staff member, or parent who makes a bullying comment to another adult should be confronted and told that such remarks are not acceptable. How in the world can students ever be persuaded to stop bullying when they witness adult bullying in the schools? Adults are physically modeling the same acts they are verbally deploring. Actions speak louder than words. When an educator is humiliated in front of students, he/she is robbed of his/her dignity and authority to manage the classroom effectively. Students are negatively impacted when this happens, and parents learn which educators they can safely attack by following the lead of others. Stopping these kinds of incidents is vital if we are to set a positive example as adults in the classrooms for students to follow.

You might say, "What can I do? I am just a teacher." Or, "I am a para-professional, (or, "I am just a school parent volunteer"); I cannot change the bullying culture at my school; it has to come from the top."

There is a lot you can do!!! You can start by assessing your own bullying behaviors and making step-by-step behavior changes. Second, you can become an *upstander*. When I train kids to be *upstanders* instead of being *bystanders*, I am empowering them to stand up for their peers! What about saying something to the person who is throwing a fellow colleague under the bus? How about confronting offensive comments in a team meeting? You could also befriend the educator who is easily left out and excluded from social activities or leave the scene when others are gossiping. Take a screenshot of something that is sent to you that disparages another peer and then report it. Challenge yourself by practicing good listening skills when someone is expressing differing opinions.

Revisiting one of my original questions, "What if we worked in an atmosphere where general kindness prevailed, where all opinions were welcomed, where respectful behaviors were the norm?"

My Challenge to You:

Do your part in promoting kindness, welcoming differing opinions, and 'living gracefully out loud' by modeling respectful behaviors. What is one behavioral change you can incorporate to foster a caring, kind, respectful, and unified culture at home and at your work?

Journal Prompt:

Visualize a typical day in your classroom, office, or school building. Imagine that everyone is being encouraging, kind, and helpful. Smiles, laughter, and joy are readily present. What interactions are occurring? Describe the tone, atmosphere, and mood. Describe your feelings.

"I am only one, but I am one. I cannot do everything, but I can do something. And I will not let what I cannot do interfere with what I can do."

— **Edward Everett Hale**, an American author, historian, and minister

Meet Erin Jones

Erin Jones has devoted her adult life to working as an award-winning educator, a winning coach, a caring mentor, a captivating speaker, an astute author, a devoted activist, and a dynamite trainer. She has taught in the most diverse communities in the nation and has been an inspiration for young people across the globe.

Erin was born in St. Paul, Minnesota, and was educated in the Netherlands at the American School of The Hague, where her parents taught. She has traveled to fourteen countries, learned to speak four languages fluently, and has become a dynamic force of positive change in the world.

In 2007, Erin received an award as the Most Innovative Foreign Language Teacher and was the Washington Milken Educator of the Year in 2008. Erin was recognized at the White House in March of 2013 as a "Champion of Change" and was the Washington State PTA's "Outstanding Educator" in 2015.

After working for two state superintendents, Erin was inspired to run for state superintendent herself in 2016. After a marginal loss by a mere 1 percent, Erin decided to leverage her experiences and pivot her career to become a motivational speaker and equity trainer in school districts, organizations, and local nonprofits. Erin challenges students, faculty, administrators, and parents to transform their losses into opportunities for growth.

Erin and her husband, James, have been married for twenty-six years and have served in ministry as youth pastors, worship team leaders, and as elders. They have three adult children, each of whom is involved in education in some manner.

Meet Erin Jones

Follow Erin Jones
@erinjonesin2016
@erinin2016
Erin Jones 2016

3

FROM LOSS TO
LIVING YOUR BEST LIFE

Erin Jones

"'For I know the plans I have for you,' declares the Lord,
'plans to prosper you and not to harm you,
plans to give you hope and a future.'"
Jeremiah 29:11

H AVE YOU BEEN ABANDONED AND REJECTED IN significant
ways? Have you lost in big, public ways? Loss, rejection,
and abandonment don't have to paralyze you from achieving
your dreams.

I was waiting in the airport for a flight to California as
the 2019 statewide election results were shared across social
media platforms and on every TV station. I was reminded of
the statewide election I had lost by less than 1 percent just
three years earlier. My loss might have been by the smallest
margin in our state that year, but there are no second-place
awards for political office.

As I walked down the halls of the airport, thinking about
the events of 2016, the entire Pepperdine women's basketball
team walked past me. I played basketball for more than thirty
years—from elementary school to recreational leagues to two
tryouts for WNBA teams. I always engage high school and
college ball players when and wherever I see them. This time
was no different.

I began a conversation with a young woman in a Pepperdine sweatshirt who was hobbling down the hall, many paces behind her teammates, a cast covering her foot and lower leg. Just as she was telling me how she injured her foot, a woman called out, "Jones, right? Your son must have graduated from Harvey Mudd by now?"

What are the chances that the Pepperdine coach had at one time been the coach for Claremont College, where nearly two years earlier I had spoken to her team while visiting my son at a partner college?

"Wow! I can't believe you still remember my name!" I said. "I didn't realize you were at Pepperdine now. Are you all headed to or home from a game?"

"We played our first game of the season last night. We lost really big by over thirty points. The ladies are pretty dejected."

The team and staff had their heads down. Many had headphones over their ears, shutting out the public.

This kind of loss I know well.

Loss, rejection, and abandonment have played powerful roles in my life. What I know from almost fifty years of life is that loss, rejection, and abandonment are real for every human being. The details of each story might be different, but one guarantee is that we all struggle and experience strife—some of our own doing and some due to the realities of life in a fallen world.

Loss began for me when I was abandoned in a hospital in St. Paul, Minnesota, on June 3, 1971. My biological mother was white. On my birth certificate, the father is named "Negro Man." I can only imagine how that went over in Minnesota, just a year before abortion would become legal.

I would start life at the Children's Home Society. I was adopted just months later by a couple from Northern Minnesota. They adopted a second biracial, unrelated boy and then chose to take us both overseas, where my father took a job at the American School of The Hague.

While I experienced loss via abandonment by my biological parents, adoption brought me into a new family who embraced me and championed my potential. They provided me with every opportunity to grow as an athlete, a student, and a musician. They connected me to a world none of us could have imagined from small-town Minnesota, where our lives began.

The event that had the greatest impact on my life took place when I was nine years old. I was a fourth grader at The American School of The Hague, where my father began teaching in 1976. My best friend that year was the daughter of the Israeli ambassador to the United Nations. Her name was Yael Ronan. The year was 1980. Israel and Palestine were at odds. Bombs and shootings were a weekly occurrence. Of course, this was long before the internet or cell phones, so Yael and her family were in constant fear of who in their families might have been injured or lost their lives in the most recent attack.

As a nine-year-old, my heart broke for Yael as she tried to navigate her painful emotions at such a young age . . . and then I discovered there was a young Palestinian boy in our school as well. Now my heart broke for the greater conflict between the two nations. For some reason, I became convinced that I (a nine-year-old, abandoned-and-then-adopted American girl) could bring peace to Israel and Palestine. I knew instinctively I would need to learn both languages—Arabic *and* Hebrew—in order to serve as a bridge between these people groups. Every lunch period I studied—Hebrew with Yael; Arabic with my friend, Najat, from Libya.

In the winter of my fourth-grade year, our school would receive a visit from the wife of Egyptian President Anwar Sadat. Egypt was in the middle of a civil war, and Mrs. Sadat had a vision much like mine—to bring peace, not only to her country but also to the entire world. She was convinced that if she could encourage small children to think about and commit to peace, we could end war globally. She decided to deliver speeches in elementary schools across the world, sharing her vision of what she believed was possible. What better place to start than the American School of The Hague, the school that served the children of most of the ambassadors and lawyers for the United Nations World Court.

Mrs. Sadat brought a special guest with her to our school. His name was John Denver. He sang several songs (including "Leaving on a Jet Plane") with our school choir, and then she delivered a speech. After the assembly, three fourth-grade students were invited to have lunch with Mrs. Sadat and John Denver, and I was one of the three.

At nine years old, I sat at a lunch table with the wife of a president and one of the most famous singers in the world. Mrs. Sadat asked each of us children how we wanted to change the world (I have since taught nine-year-olds and raised three of my own; I can assure you most nine-year-olds are *not* thinking about changing the world).

"Mrs. Sadat," I said at one point, "I am going to bring peace to Israel and Palestine. I am teaching myself to speak Hebrew and Arabic."

Instead of laughing at this precocious nine-year-old, Mrs. Sadat looked me dead in the eyes and said these words, "Erin, you are a world-changer."

She didn't tell me I *would be* a world-changer. She told me I *was* a world-changer.

From that moment on, I lived my life with purpose. I knew if I were to honor Mrs. Sadat's words, I needed to seek every day to become the best version of myself. I knew that no matter what happened—what losses or challenges I encountered—I could not stop moving forward.

Most of the students who attended the American School of The Hague planned to attend college in the United States after graduation. It was an expectation, even for students who were not American by birth. I followed in the footsteps of every student who had gone before me.

My first choice was Princeton. I was accepted there in March 1989, but the college never looked at my financial aid paperwork to see I was the child of educators. All the admissions office saw was the name of the exclusive private high school where my father taught, and they assumed I was wealthy like my classmates. Princeton would offer me only a $1,000 annual scholarship, even though I had an almost-perfect GPA, great SAT scores, was the captain and MVP for three varsity sports, and played two instruments in the band. I was devastated the night my parents sat me down to tell me my first choice college was not a possibility on their budget.

My world shattered.

I had done everything I had been told to do and more.

Just weeks later, I received a letter from Bryn Mawr College informing me they wanted to offer me a significant scholarship. Although I had received several full-ride scholarships to small colleges, none were as prestigious as Bryn Mawr, so I made my decision to begin school there in fall 1989, sight unseen.

I left The Netherlands and came to the United States with dreams of studying pre-law or world languages and then pursuing a law degree at an Ivy League university. I planned to return home to The Netherlands to work at the United Nations World Court, either as an international lawyer or as an interpreter.

Although I was not going to my dream college, I still had high hopes for my future. I had always worked hard, always accomplished my goals, always been surrounded by champions. That was about to change.

College was not an empowering place.

I was one of ten Black students in a predominantly white institution.

I was the daughter of classroom teachers, surrounded by the daughters of royalty, business executives, and big-time lawyers.

I was a two-sport athlete at a college that cared nothing for athletics.

The college was located in a town that saw Black people as worthy only of working in the service industry. I was often called names when I left campus. I was followed in every store by security, who saw me as a threat. Not even a mile from campus, a sign was posted on the edge of a private cricket club stating, "No coloreds or Jews allowed here" (this sign was not removed until 2012, by the way).

I did not know how to be in that space. I began to struggle with an eating disorder. I had suicidal thoughts. I wanted to disappear from the planet.

Through a powerful experience on a basketball court the summer after my freshman year, in the depths of depression, I would "find God." However, my struggles did not end. Walking with God, I would learn over the next thirty years that struggle just *is*. Struggle is inevitable. Struggle is life. Even the Son of God knew struggle. He was rejected and abandoned while on the earth. Even He endured suffering and loss.

Sometimes struggle is personal—between you and God, or you and a spouse, or you and a friend; sometimes the struggle is feeling marginalized or excluded because you look or sound different. Sometimes the struggle is big and public—a financial scandal, or filing for bankruptcy, or losing a statewide election.

I made the decision to run for state superintendent of schools in 2016. Having never run for office before, I was thought by many to have no chance. I had doubters from the very beginning. Although I won the primary, I lost in the general election by less than 1 percent. When I lost, so many people were ready to support me through the depression they expected to come. They knew how much time, energy, and money I had invested in the campaign, and how publicly I had been maligned.

I knew from the beginning I was walking in God's purpose for my life. I was not deterred by my loss. At nineteen, when I was a college student who had just found God, I knew God had made me just as I was and was taking me on a journey to be a champion for young people. I was just as sure, almost thirty years later, I could be a champion for young people, whether elected to political office or not.

The last three years following my campaign loss have represented the *best* season of my life. The day I conceded the race to my opponent, I reached out to my teacher friends on social media and asked if anyone had a classroom I could visit and share my personal story. I was in a classroom the very next day talking about the power of trying hard things, being willing to lose, getting back up, and moving forward. Each year since my loss, I have spoken to an average of 150,000 students and 50,000 adults. In August 2019 alone, I was invited to speak in eight states.

Who could have known such a devastating loss could lead to such incredible opportunity?!

I have learned a great deal from and about loss.

Loss has been a perpetual part of my life—from sports to school to relationships to politics.

When I ran into the Pepperdine women's basketball coach in the airport and she asked if I had something I could share with her players about overcoming loss, I knew I was more than prepared. They had lost *a* game. This was not an end. This was just *a* step on their journey. This was a learning opportunity.

For more than twenty-five years, I have prayed this prayer, "God, let all the painful things I have experienced become an inspiration for others, hope for the possibility in their futures."

I didn't have much time with the Pepperdine ladies before they had to get on their plane to head home, but I have spent a lot of time thinking about my losses lately in preparation for the writing of this chapter. Here are some of the nuggets I shared with the team that I hope will bless you:

1. Loss is inevitable. We all experience loss and suffering at some point. It is not the loss and suffering that define you but *how* you respond. Your response is your choice. (I'm not saying it's easy, but you are in control of how you respond, not anyone else.)

2. Loss doesn't have to paralyze you. Loss is just a reminder that you have more things to learn, more challenges to push through, different doors to investigate.

3. Loss is often not as much about the closing of a door as it is the opening of a door you didn't know existed.

The ladies' faces lit up. I could see a bit of hope restored in them and in the coaching staff. We took a group photo, and they boarded their plane. It was clear this encounter was no accident. I was meant to be in the airport at just that moment.

My losses have not been pain-free. Some have required counseling and coaching to overcome, but each loss has opened the door to amazing opportunities—from acquiring new adoptive parents (who are my heroes) to becoming an award-winning educator to starting my own speaking and training business that has given me freedom like I have never experienced before.

My losses have influenced how I show up for the students and educators I get to work with now as a consultant. As educators, we have opportunities to experience failure and rejection every day—from bombing a lesson, not connecting to a colleague or student, not earning National Boards the first time we try, or not being selected for that committee or leadership opportunity we want.

As you move forward in your career, consider these strategies I try to live by to move through loss into success:

- It is important to remind yourself on a regular basis *why* you got involved in education, why you are in this particular role, and why you have chosen to work in this location. When your *why* is big enough, it will sustain you through the most difficult of circumstances.

- When you have a bad teaching day on the day of your evaluation and don't get the score you think you deserve, or you don't get the marks necessary to earn your National Board certificate, do not let it paralyze or define you. See the score as an opportunity to practice those skills you are trying to teach your students—perseverance, grit, and growth-mindset.

- Be intentional about who gets to be around you. Seek out mentors who have skill in an area you are seeking to develop. Seek opportunities to serve those who are earlier in their careers. Eliminate relationships with those who are constantly negative.

- Find quotes or passages of scripture that inspire you. During my darkest hours, Psalm 139 has been my reminder that God made me exactly as I am and that who I am is more than enough. Jeremiah 29:11 is my reminder that God has good things for my future. Is there a quote or Scripture you can commit to reading each day to remind you of your purpose and destiny? Start there with reprogramming your mind to believe you can and will overcome.

Loss and rejection are inevitable. The beauty is that life occurs in seasons. If you find yourself in a difficult season, know that a new season *is* coming!

My Challenges to You:

Identify a current struggle in your life—big or small. Take a moment to be thankful for what you do have at the moment, what is working in your life. Then reflect on your life purpose and determine whether this struggle is one meant to push you to persevere, to learn new skills, or to change your direction . . . and then keep moving forward, one day at a time.

Find a quote that speaks to you. Print it out or write it up, and put it on something you look at every day (a mirror, a door, your cell phone screen). Make yourself read the quote at least once a day for the next month, until it becomes part of you.

Journal Prompts:

What is the reason you got into education? If you were to explain your decision to your students or to a group of families, practice writing out what you would say.

Identify one of the greatest losses, rejections, or failures you have ever faced. Reflect on how you have grown from that experience. What did you learn? What else could you do to use the experience to your benefit?

What is the greatest challenge you have had to overcome? What were the strategies or relationships you used to move into a new season? What were your greatest lessons learned?

4
MOTHER AS EDUCATOR

Erin Jones

"For you created my inmost being; you knit me together in my mother's womb. I praise you because I am fearfully and wonderfully made; your works are wonderful, I know that full well. My frame was not hidden from you when I was made in the secret place, when I was woven together in the depths of the earth. Your eyes saw my unformed body; all the days ordained for me were written in your book before one of them came to be. How precious to me are your thoughts, God! How vast is the sum of them!"
Psalms 139:13-17 NIV

W HAT IF BECOMING A MOTHER CHANGES HOW we educate, and what if how we educate changes our "mothering"? I never planned to be either—mother or educator.

My parents were both career educators—Dad for more than forty years; Mom for more than thirty. I had both of them as teachers . . . *twice*. My uncle was a community college professor for almost fifty years. Two of his three boys are educators—one a professor, one a high school teacher.

I was adopted as a baby by the Adamsons. I did not expect to follow in the footsteps of anyone in the Adamson family.

I knew as a young student (by nine years old) that I wanted to change the world. My parents both taught at the

American School of The Hague. The United Nations World Court was in our backyard, meaning I was surrounded by the children of international lawyers and State Department officials. My parents raised me to believe I could change the world in a significant way, like those around me who were writing law or prosecuting international criminals. I had every plan to become an international lawyer or an interpreter, since I was fluent in four languages by sixteen.

That was, until I arrived in the United States for college in 1989 and realized quickly that students who looked like me and attended public schools in the United States had not received the same quality of education I had received in The Netherlands, nor were they surrounded by champions as I had been.

I learned about the difference in expectations for students who looked like me late in my freshman year. I learned this by being called names while walking through my college town, being doubted for my abilities by educators, and by being expected to score points on the field or on the court but not in the classroom. I learned this after I had begun to wish I could just disappear, when I began to doubt myself and my potential in serious ways for the first time in my life. One day in the midst of deep depression, I happened upon a basketball court miles outside of my college town where everyone looked like me, where every young man on the court with me had given up on school.

After a day of playing basketball, I would ask the four boys still sitting in the park, "What's your dream for the future, if you're not going to get your high school diploma?"

"We don't expect to live to be twenty-one. Why would we dream about the future?"

That was the moment I realized for the first time that my parents had been world-changers as teachers. I realized I was both white and black for a reason. I was an athlete and an academic for a reason. I made the long walk back to my college campus knowing my life had just changed in ways I could not even comprehend. I knew I was not returning home, that I would spend a lifetime invested in young people in the nation of my birth.

I began volunteering with young people as soon as possible my sophomore year of college. At the same time, I was experiencing incredible pain during my menstrual cycles, was told I had a severe case of endometriosis and would likely never have my own children. I had never dated seriously and was pretty convinced I would be single for the rest of my life. My family would be my colleagues and students.

The summer after my sophomore year, I met James in an academic program hosted at Boston University. He and I were engaged within the next year and married only months after my graduation from college. He was in graduate school at Notre Dame studying political science. Although we hoped to have our own children, we knew the odds were slim. We began talking early about adopting children. I am adopted. Three of his siblings are adopted.

And then one day, while I was playing indoor soccer, I trapped a ball with my stomach and doubled over with pain. Regardless of what I had been told by several doctors, my husband knew without a doubt I was pregnant and took me immediately to a crisis pregnancy facility to do a pregnancy test. Miraculously, I was pregnant. As if that was not a big enough shock, when I stopped nursing our first son after eighteen months, I became pregnant with our second.

Having our own biological children changed everything.

I had always thought of myself as a career-woman more than a mother. My plan after both pregnancies was to take the traditional nine weeks off and then return to the classroom. With our first child in tow, the private school where I taught offered to hire my husband as well (since we both had degrees in English). He would take over for me while I was on maternity leave. I would return to take over, and our son would go into a home daycare.

After nine weeks, though, I found I couldn't bear the thought of leaving our son during the day. I was suddenly aware there were things only I could provide that no daycare could. We worked out an arrangement—my husband taught half the day, and I taught the other half. With the second child, it made no sense to work at all. The daycare costs alone would equal what I would make as a teacher.

I decided to stay home. My husband had since become a full-time youth pastor for the pastor under whom he had been raised as a child, so now we had a couple dozen "additional children." One day during the summer, I was driving my kids to a friend's house for a play date, and I happened to pass a Christian school going out of business. I am not sure what prompted me to stop and go into the building, but I felt drawn. When I got inside and started looking around, I found two people sitting in a classroom looking exhausted.

"Want to buy a school for $200?"

An entire school?

The two educators sold me all that was left of the school: several tables, chairs, shelving units, games, textbooks, workbooks, and manipulatives—all for $200.

I had already been thinking about homeschooling my children like many of the other mothers in my church. Now I had everything I needed to make that a reality.

We turned our finished garage into a "home school." That was when the challenge of being a mother-teacher began, along with challenges I hadn't anticipated. My husband and I had read to our children since they were in vitro. We visited the public library once a week for children's reading hour. Although the kids colored and used scissors and glue at church, these were not skills on which I had focused. Now that we had "a school" in our garage, I felt obligated to do more "school stuff."

I watched as my older son struggled to hold a pencil or scissors for any length of time. Not only were his fine motor skills atrocious; he would complain of pain in his hand after trying to color or write for more than thirty seconds. Something was wrong, but I didn't know what. I had never seen anything like this before. I figured I would just have to work longer and harder with him. I was glad we had invested in this school to give him the additional support he was going to need.

Our youngest son was singing the alphabet and recognizing letters by the age of three. He was using polysyllabic words by four or five . . . correctly, in context, after hearing them once. You could see him "try out" words in public places, obviously pleased with himself when adults were impressed.

The more we worked in our "garage school," the more I began to recognize differences between the boys. The older one struggled to sit in a chair for long, although, even at five, he could have full-length conversations with any adult about sports. The younger one could sit for hours coloring or putting together puzzles, and he insisted he was going to teach himself how to read, "Mommy, stop teaching me [to read]. I'm going to do this myself."

And then summer came, and the other children began to show up at our door . . .

"Ummm . . . Miss Lady, can I come use the bathroom?"

"Miss Lady, do you have any snacks?"

"Miss Lady, can we come play with your kids?"

My children were the youngest in our neighborhood. At first I could not figure out why the older kids wanted to be in our house. Then I discovered almost every one of the parents worked during the day. The neighborhood appeared "middle class" (the houses were all fairly new and spacious), but the reality was that everyone had purchased homes above their means. No one had money for childcare. The practice was to either leave children alone at home or (worse) lock them out of the house and tell them to find somewhere to play until Mom and/or Dad came home from work.

Could I have called Child Protective Services (CPS)? Sure, but I knew from my few years in public school that often those calls did not accomplish anything but arouse parental anger. I did not want to be "that lady" in our neighborhood. I realized quickly these parents were doing the best they could, and I felt obligated to take action. That summer I opened the school in my garage to the children of our neighborhood. I knew that if the children in my neighborhood were unable to read, write, and do math, trouble was coming . . . I knew that investing in the young people in our community was an investment in the safety of my children and the future of our neighborhood.

I had fifteen children in my "home school" that summer. The students ranged in age from my children (three and five) to twelve years old. The school was open from eight in the morning until four in the afternoon. My church provided me with supplies to make a basic lunch each day. Starbucks donated day-old pastries every day that we could use for breakfast or afternoon snacks. An elementary teacher who attended our church offered to join me to teach reading a couple times a week. We had academic time, during which I read aloud to them and the students learned basic math facts and phonics, and practiced writing complete sentences. We played board games. We went on visits to the park.

And then summer was over, as soon as it had begun.

As much as I was reminded each day in our "summer school" of my own children's struggles—our oldest continued to struggle holding a pencil and often needed regular reminders to stay on task; our youngest was determined to learn most things on his own, to be on his own. I also became much more aware of the importance of the messages we as adults send children about education and "academic things." Most of the other children did not have anyone else reading to them or doing academic activities beyond the school day. All of their skills were below what I imagined to be "at-grade-level."

We kept our oldest at home for kindergarten that year, concerned about his readiness to start public school, considering his struggles with writing. The following year, we decided trained elementary educators might be better prepared to meet his needs, so he started first grade with his peers. Looking back, I don't know that this was a good decision. I don't think he learned any new academic skills that year, but he definitely learned some negative coping skills (how to distract from anything he didn't want to do; how to get kicked out of his classroom by singing during quiet times). Once his younger brother was ready for kindergarten, we made the decision to change schools and give him a fresh start with his brother in a new environment.

I was feeling the call to return to the classroom, to use my skills to bless more children than just my own. I took a job teaching middle school at the feeder middle school just a couple miles from our house. An amazing opportunity opened that required a French teacher for a new Language Immersion program. As the only fluent French speaker the superintendent knew, I was recruited for the position and given the green light to design the program I wanted. I was able to interview and select students for my program. What an incredible opportunity and confirmation that I was exactly where I was meant to be.

I wish things were that simple—a clear path forward.

Our oldest continued to have a hard time in school. The first few weeks that year, he came home almost daily talking about how stupid he felt. He could not articulate to us why, but every day he walked through the door looking more discouraged than the day before. By the third week of school, I knew we needed a parent-teacher conference. Here were the words of his teacher in that first face-to-face encounter, "You know, I thought your son was stupid for the first three weeks of school," (Yes, she said *those* words) "and then I realized he must have a learning disability."

It turned out he did have a learning disability, but to say that, to say *those* words . . .

I would never forget her words, and he would never (not even now at twenty-five) forget how she made him feel.

It took two years after that meeting, a change of school districts, and a great deal of research and testing to have our oldest diagnosed with something called *dysgraphia*. In simple terms, dysgraphia is the written form of dyslexia. My son's brain and his hand do not connect. No matter how many hours we spent practicing penmanship, he was never able to form letters that were legible. Dysgraphia also affects organizational and linear thinking, so traditional school was a very painful process for him.

By fourth grade, our son would finally qualify for a 504 Plan, which allowed him to access accommodations and receive additional supports, such as extended time for testing and the use of a laptop for written activities. As a fellow educator, I insisted on meeting with teachers, from fifth grade beyond, before the school year started each year, hoping to help them understand his disability and give them practical strategies to support him. All too often, even with my intervention as a parent, he did not receive the necessary accommodations. At times, he had teachers who really tried. At other times, he had teachers who insisted he needed to be treated like everyone else, because to do otherwise was unfair (by the way, a 504 is a legal document). He graduated high school by the skin of his teeth, with the help of every adult in his life (including my parents, who retired to the United States when he was a sophomore in high school, and a choir teacher who recognized his brilliance).

Our youngest son started public school as a kindergartner. Remember, he had asked me not to teach him to read. I was ashamed to send him to school the first day. I even apologized to the teacher for not being a good educator-parent. I will never forget her call home that night, "Mrs. Jones? This is Mrs. King, Israel's kindergarten teacher. I know you told me this morning your son could not read, but I think you are wrong. He walked into the classroom and informed me that my 'September Box' was not in the right place on the shelves. He was obviously able to read 'August' and 'October' to know it was missing."

We would realize quickly that our youngest had special academic abilities. He picked up new information and skills at a much more accelerated pace than his peers, but he also struggled to engage socially with children his age. By the time he was in second grade, I suspected he had what is now called "high-functioning autism," but what I had only heard as "Asperger's" until that time. We fought that diagnosis for many years, worried about what would happen to a Black boy with that label. We were worried he would be placed in special education, instead of the Gifted programs we knew would better suit him.

Unfortunately, we moved quite a bit during his early years of elementary school, and he was forced to take the Gifted test in each new district. In one district, the administrator came into the lobby, where all parents and tested students were waiting for results, and announced loudly enough for others to hear, "I think your son must have cheated on this test. There's no way he scored this high on his own."

The beauty of people with autism (I think it is a gift) is their lack of filters. Without skipping a beat, my son responded, "Well, sir, I will just take the test again and score higher."

I was livid. I knew exactly what the accusation was about—this was the only Black child testing. A Black boy could not possibly be this smart. *Oh, yes he could.* Our youngest son would go on to get one wrong on the math SAT (as a high school junior, having not taken a prep class) and would earn a significant scholarship to Harvey Mudd College, one of the most selective math and science colleges in the nation. He is now pursuing a master's degree in Mixed Media at the University of Southern California.

As a mother and educator, I found these experiences painful. There were a couple instances where my husband and I had evidence for a court case but, as fellow educators in a district, we were in a position, as colleagues, where filing suit would have created a difficult dynamic. Looking back, now that our sons have graduated from high school and have moved into young adulthood, I wonder if we made the right decisions. They have both paid a price for ways they were treated by the very schools my husband and I committed to serving. Conversely, they have both also benefitted from positive relationships and encounters in school spaces. In spite of the ways our oldest son experienced school, he coaches high school football with his father at the local high school from which he graduated. Our youngest son plans to use his graduate degree to develop online video games for use in educational spaces.

Having now worked as a classroom teacher and an administrator for more than two decades, I realize all our struggles as a family can benefit others. As a consultant now, I get to stand in the gap to both help the system better serve students like the ones I raised and to help parents understand how to ensure their students get what they need—when it is worth a legal battle and when it is best to move through the chain of command.

Here are some lessons I have learned through the process that I hope will benefit you as both educator and parent:

1. Educating a classroom of children is *hard* work!

2. Every child has a different learning style. Those differences are both a challenge and a gift.

3. Every child has at least one talent (and often many). It is our job as educators to find and nurture their brilliance.

4. If we teach each child as if s/he is our own, as if they are equally valuable to the world as our own, we will raise our standards for instruction.

5. Building relationships with students is critical to determine the most effective instructional strategies.

6. When you struggle to meet the needs of a student, take time to meet with the student's family. There is always a *why* students behave in ways that do not work within your classroom structure. I have yet to find a parent or family member who doesn't know something useful about the student.

7. When your own personal child struggles with a teacher, have compassion for that adult, but do whatever is necessary to stand up for your child and speak up for their needs. Your child is likely not the only one struggling with the teacher, and others might not know how to advocate in the ways you do.

We must choose every day to grow . . . and in so doing model for our children, our students, and our colleagues to do the same.

My Challenge to You:

Think about the students or staff in your school/district. Picture in your mind the one with whom you struggle to connect the most. Imagine that child/adult is now living in your home. How might you treat that person differently if you perceived them as "your own"?

What would you do in your classroom if you had a student with dysgraphia, dyslexia, or autism? Do you have the tools in your toolbox to serve students with different learning needs? Is there a local training source you could attend to at least develop some basic awareness?

What would you have done differently for one of your children, if you could go back in time?

Journal Prompts:

What changed about your instruction once you had children?

Describe the most difficult experience you have had trying to engage another educator on behalf of your child.

Is there a strategy that worked for one of your own children that you tried with a student or with a whole classroom?

Meet Jenny Severson, EdD

Dr. Jenny Severson is a rare talent. Over the past twenty-five years, as a respected and sought-out speaker, Jenny has presented worldwide to thousands of professional educators, parents, and administrators. Audiences rave about the meaningful learning experiences Dr. Severson creates with her upbeat energy, authentic communication style, and gift for explaining difficult-to-understand concepts. Dr. Severson is Brené Brown Dare to Lead trained and utilizes her unique vision, years of experience, and evidence-based research in her work.

Jenny is an in-demand coach, trainer, and consultant for schools, corporations, churches, and nonprofit organizations. She delivers skyrocketing results by improving the social and emotional skills of teams and transforming school cultures. She is revered for emphasizing the importance of interconnectedness and for her commitment to re-humanization in the workplace.

Dr. Severson's signature approach and warm presence support people in integrating their personal and professional lives so that they are freed, fueled, and inspired to bring their best selves to both work and home.

Jenny is a globally sought-out and passionate conference speaker who has worked in forty-seven states and seventeen countries. By inviting Dr. Severson into your school or organization, you will experience transformation and revitalization. You will also encounter a refreshing perspective that will have lasting impact.

Jenny is the author of *The 180-degree Teacher Turn Around: How to Be* Grateful *Every Day* and, *The* Gratitude *Calendar.* Writing *Thrive* with her Speaker Sisters has been balm for Jenny's soul.

She, her husband Todd Johnson, and their three growing children live in Minnesota.

Meet Jenny Severson, EdD

Follow Jenny Severson, EdD
608-347-7325
jennyseverson.com
jeniferjseverson@gmail.com
Twitter @Severson_J
insta: dr.jenny.severson
Facebook: Jenny Severson

5
SELF-CARE AND GRATITUDE AS AN EDUCATOR

Dr. Jenny Severson

"Heal me, O Lord and I shall be healed; save me, and I shall be saved, for you are my praise."
Jeremiah 17:14

"Then he touched their eyes (of the blind men) and said, 'According to your faith let it be done to you.'"
Matthew 9:29

W E ALL HAVE A MOMENT IN TIME that defines us—a story. What is your story?

I will share part of my story here. It is one chapter of my life I own whole-heartedly and that I am truly grateful to share. This story is one that defines how I will live the rest of my life.

The facts:

- I found a small lump on the left side of my breast while stretching in October 2017.
- I woke up the next day and knew something wasn't right.
- I had the lump biopsied in November 2017.
- I found out December 26, 2017, I had breast cancer.

- On January 2, my husband, Todd, and I met with our doctors.

- On January 12, I had surgery to remove the mass (the surgery was a success; we caught it early and nothing had spread).

- The mass was sent for testing, and we waited for the results.

- On February 1, my dad died. He was seventy-four years old.

- On February 7, we held his funeral.

- On February 21 (which would have been my dad's seventy-fifth birthday), I found out from my doctors that it would be wise for me to do both chemotherapy and radiation due to the mass that was removed and the cells being very chaotic . . . I had an Oncatype of 28 (under 18 avoids chemo, in my case).

- On February 26, I started chemotherapy.

- On March 14, all my hair fell out.

- I was bald, sick, and nearly dead (at least that is how I felt) for the next three months.

- In March, April, and May I went through more chemo, illness, and navigating life.

- I finished radiation on Monday, July 28, and moved back to Minnesota on September 7, 2018.

This list neglects to mention we had no close circle of friends or family around us during this time because several months earlier we had just moved to a new state (fourteen hours away). We had moved for my husband's job—a two-year assignment.

Life felt pretty dark.

Lonely, afraid, and with no sense of belonging, I was shut down to those around me much of the time. I now know I was in self-protection mode.

After March 2018, I knew I had a *very* good chance of coming out OK, which was hugely helpful. In fact, by taking the actions we did, there is a very low, single-digit chance of recurrence compared to 40 percent for those who get no treatment. Numbers can create relief. However, there was a long time (December 26–March 26, to be exact) when I wasn't clear on what my outcomes would be.

This chapter is about some of the action steps I took and still take daily to stay with what I know to be the "next right things" to do. I did the research with my doctors and learned about a protocol that has helped more than 865,000 women with my type of breast cancer, who have followed the protocol completely, successfully thrive for thirty to forty years after treatment. I'll admit, that news helped me—*a lot*. It made me see I was going to get a second chance at life.

So, what would I do with that new knowledge? How would I start to take care of myself so that I could live the life God intended for me? As I explored the difficult time I had experienced over the previous year, I realized that what lifted me out of this lonely, anxious, and dark experience were the following:

- God's grace and forgiveness.

- Faith, gratitude, curiosity, and optimism.

- Connection and belonging to my immediate family and to powerful communities of hope.

- Living in a spirit of simplicity and neutrality, with moments of newness and fun.

So, what was there to be grateful for in this series of events?

Actually, there was *a lot*.

In fact, more than ever, I felt carried and surrounded by God's love, direction, and presence during this time. Often my face was flat on the floor as I prayed and asked for healing and gratitude. For example, at my dad's funeral, there was no way I could tell anyone about my medical situation. I couldn't even process all the trauma I was experiencing. Instead of talking to others, I talked to God. I needed to get into God's Word every day in order to rewire and train my brain to have a new perspective. I had gotten off course, and my journey to healing would only be attained through God's grace, and my gratitude and optimism.

I can now say with certainty that getting cancer, fighting cancer, and beating cancer has resulted in living my life differently. As strange as it might seem, my struggle with cancer is one of the best things that has ever happened to me. Yes, I am grateful for breast cancer, because it is teaching me so much about my life. The life I have ahead of me is a gift each and every day. When you stare at your own death, you realize how fragile things are and, yet, more importantly, how strong God is in the midst.

Before cancer I was hustling, performing, pretending, looking for approval in others, gaining titles and status, running through airports nonstop, lacking in self-care, overweight in pounds, heavy in spirit, overwhelmed, and overextended.

Have you ever felt this way?

I now realize I have a daily choice to not go back there. I pray every day that I stay centered on God's words and truths, and that I never go back to the external, self-will-run-riot-pace-of-life people pleasing, and address boundaries daily! I keep rituals in place to keep listening for God's direction and reminding myself of my story. I cannot be casual about boundaries anymore. My life matters and so does yours.

Owning my story and my life's path really gives God the glory because He walked me through it. When I was alone, He was present. His scripture and words filled my heart with calm. When fear arose, I was able to see His path and trust in the revelation of His story for me.

When we have gifts and talents, which all of us do, and we use them in accord rather than discord with all those things and people around us, we are blessed with gratitude and optimism.

The question is how do *you* stay centered on the action and mindset of living the life God has called you to today? What is the centering action that guides you there? For me, the answer is gratitude. When gratitude is not present, I can be optimistic. What is there to look forward to? Gratitude and optimism are like sister emotions. They walk hand-in-hand to connect us to love, peace, calm, clarity of purpose . . . our True North. This daily action plan around gratitude is my ongoing story, future, and passion—to instill in each of us a sense that God has placed us here to see what is good and to feel heaven on earth.

Here are the words of Jeremiah again: "Heal me, O Lord and I shall be healed; save me, and I shall be saved, for you are my praise (Jeremiah 17:14, NIV)."

Then, also, again, as in Matthew 9:29: "Then he touched the eyes of the blind men and said, "According to your faith let it be done to you."

Take a deep breath. *Ahhh.* Breathe in gratitude and healing. Gratitude and healing. As these words wash over you and soak deeply into your being, they give you a sense of peace and joy.

Although gratitude and healing go hand-in-hand, we sometimes separate them. This happens because neurobiologically they operate in different parts of our brain. Upsets, unmet expectations, trauma, and hard conversations affect us. Our body responds and keeps score. Ever had an argument? Why is it the next day I think of my best comebacks? That is part of our wiring! How our brains are wired changes based on how we attend to ourselves. What we do and do not do every day impact how we perform, how we show up, and how we connect to those around us.

Consider what happens when you are in an argument. In the moment of the argument, your brain's working memory is in flight/flee mode. Downshifting into fight/flee happens as quickly as seven seconds! Sometimes days *after* the argument (depending on the severity), you probably come up with better, more rational thinking, but not always in the moment. The work of learning how to engage effectively in difficult conversations requires lots of circling back and committing to relationships.

This chapter is about my story and how I fit into God's story. This chapter is a testimony to His divine presence and love. It is also a tool kit for self-care that I use each day.

Here we will address *why* (relevance) and *how* (actionable strategies) that I want to pay attention to. You might as well do it in your own self-care journey as an educator.

What if you could be across from me right now, chatting over coffee or tea?

I would want to know your story—not all the awards and accolades, the achievements (although those are nice), but what keeps you up at night? Where have you failed? What bothers you? What makes you discontent? Where do you want to grow? What type of margin of rest is in your daily life?

Like me, your fears, victories, and plans for the future rest in your experiences, struggles, and victories today. We say we want to be vulnerable, but vulnerability does not come easy for most people. We want to know we are not alone in the struggle, that we can find our way through adversity toward solutions. None of us wants to stay stuck! I believe that!

What this book is about are both the struggle and the gift of processing toward solutions. The process is never-ending. The process is about humility, courage, and doing the next right thing. The process is our journey as educators, parents, and people. I believe that process starts with gratitude.

Did you know that if you keep a gratitude journal for six weeks, you will see at least a 23 percent increase in energy, 31 percent higher productivity, and 40 percent likelihood of improved longevity (Schawbel, 2013).[1] Gratitude, like anything we focus on, alerts our reticular activating system—what we pay attention to grows. Where our attention goes, the energy goes, and flows! For example, ever purchased a new car? Purse? Shoes? Once you do, you see them everywhere. Your brain has picked out a common point. The science and facts pertinent to how our brains operate just give us more evidence for being intentional about our thoughts and words.

Let's actually take action on being grateful right now. Use the lines provided to respond to the following questions:

What are you grateful for today? Name one to five things:

_____

_____

_____

_____

_____

Why?
Be detailed.

_____

_____

_____

_____

_____

What are you looking forward to?
Share the details.

_____

_____

_____

_____

_____

Gratitude is essential because, if you are like me, you have taken *a lot* for granted.

What do I mean by that?

Well, stop for a second . . . you are breathing, you have shelter, you have warmth or cool air around you. Maybe you have a college degree, a job you love. Maybe you are reading this on a computer. You have lighting, a window to the outside world. You have freedom. You live in a democracy. There might be sun or rain or snow outside, but life is happening. Things are alive and moving. How we respond to these realities shapes our wiring and our brain chemistry.

Please hear this fact—gratitude is *not* natural. In fact, we are hard-wired for anger, fear, disgust, sadness, joy, and surprise . . . but not optimism, gratitude, kindness, humility (Ekman, 2011).[2] Those habits are *learned* and traceable every day when we direct attention to them.

Right now, before we go any further, write down three more things you are grateful for or optimistic about. Ready, set, go!

1. _____

2. _____

3. _____

Great work!

This next section is about the tool kit of an educator who puts self-care first. We can only assist and be of maximum service to others when our own cup is full.

Again, this is part of my daily action plan. It's not that I do it perfectly by any means, but it's a process . . . a journey, and it provides me clear direction, action, and fuels a sense of calm, clear thinking, and my True North.

This daily action plan around gratitude is my ongoing story, future, and passion—to instill in each of us a sense that God has placed us here to see what is good, to feel heaven on earth.

Facts: Unless we have solid boundaries and a sense of self, we will get run over by life's demands. Saying yes to too many things: I was an overworked teacher, principal, presenter, and mom . . . but we can choose for it to be different! Every day!

And, since I like *yes*, I now say yes—first to my faith and well-being! We must learn to say yes to taking care of ourselves—if we don't, then who will? If not now, when?

Don't wait for a crisis to get going on these values. Don't

make your health someone else's problem. That fact drives me! We have to remember we have a choice and we need accountability to keep our health and well-being central to our lives.

In her recent book, *Fair Play*, author Eve Rodsky analyzed more than four hundred articles and found that, no matter the situation, women do two-thirds of the workload in families and marriages, and the solution is not blaming or shaming your partner; it starts with boundaries.[3] Boundaries mean what is OK and what is not OK. Start with yourself and see the ripple effect of your choices.

Jenny's Daily Action Plan:

1. Gratitude! I create a gratitude list every day—five items minimum.

Examples from today: fresh white snow outside my window, bright yellow sun, blue skies, three healthy children, a thriving work life, connection to God, and my fellow Speaker Sisters.

2. Food plan. Nutrition: Have you ever thought about what you eat as if your life depends on it? Yikes, sounds pretty serious and yet, it is . . . for me, anyway. It took me almost heading to the grave early to start actually paying attention to what I was eating. I was undisciplined. I used food as a reward. I ate when I was bored, all kinds of odd stuff. We live in an obese culture. It doesn't have to be the norm. Most people have some way they numb out. For me, it was food. Today I choose differently, three times a day; when I eat, it is intentional now, and in the healthy lane.

Our standard American diet is killing us, literally. Watch *What the Health* on Netflix as a resource. Also, let's get really honest—some of you, like me, would benefit from really looking at the impact food is having on your mindset, energy, and gratitude. If you are anything like me, you over-ate in the past. I did this because my thinking was off (not grateful), and negative thinking is like a gateway drug toward killing off what is good in our lives. Determine if this is an area with which you struggle; if not, move on! You got this!

3. Integrity. I want the honesty, freedom, and happiness that come from following what I said I would do. Stop making yourself wrong by overdoing it. Over-commitment and under-deliver invite two pests: hurry and indecision.

4. Centering Prayer. When faced with upset: pause. Breathe. Ask for guidance. Pray. Slow down enough to process the situation, feeling, or circumstance. My centering prayer fellowship and the app *Calm*[4] have changed my life. Even basketball superstar LeBron James has a section of meditations on *Calm*. Give it a try. Take the time; you will not regret it!

5. Feed your brain positive upbeat messages. Think about your classroom or workspace. What is it "speaking" to you? What messages is it sending to your brain? Hot tip: Post a prayer, words that guide you. Take time to pause, think, and see what direction you are heading into.

Here are two examples I have posted:

"Make careful exploration of who you are and the work you have been given, and then sink yourself into that. Do not be impressed with yourself. Do not compare yourself with others. Each of you must take responsibility for doing the creative best you can with your own life." (Galatians 6:45 MSG)

Psalm 23:1-6

"The LORD is my shepherd;
I shall not want.
He makes me lie down in green pastures;
He leads me beside quiet waters.

He restores my soul;
He guides me in the paths of righteousness
for the sake of His name.
Even though I walk through the valley of the shadow of
death,
I will fear no evil, for You are with me;
Your rod and Your staff, they comfort me.
You prepare a table before me
in the presence of my enemies.
You anoint my head with oil; my cup overflows.
Surely goodness and mercy will follow me
all the days of my life,
and I will dwell in the house of the LORD forever.

6. Decide. Make an action plan—decide to do just the gratitude list, for example—and let the rest go. Doing too much 'creates hurry'. Remember, hurry and indecision are gratitude killers. They ruin any form of peace because you aren't meant to be a "human doing"; rather, you are meant to live as a "human being."

7. Believe in Hope. The definition of *hope* means confident expectation for something good to happen. Hope causes us to believe the promises of God. I decide to believe the promises of God. I decide to love. Why? Because what *you* say in your head drops down into your heart. The body keeps score and runs through those neural pathways into every cell in your body. Ask yourself: What are you believing about you, your life, your future?

Do I believe my best work is ahead of me? I have a sign posted with this question in front of my desk. It reminds me to stay focused on today and optimistic about what's ahead instead of dwelling on missed opportunities and past experiences.

8. Community.

Definitions:

a. A group of people living in the same place or having a particular characteristic in common.

b. A feeling of fellowship with others as a result of sharing common attitudes, interests, and goals. "The sense of community that organized religion can provide." (Google, 2020)

In my experience, the move that took us away from our friends and family devastated me. On the outside, I put on a happy face, invited people over, tried to connect at church and in women's groups, and it just wasn't working. I learned that you cannot replicate decades of friendships in one year. Value your communities! Consider:

- What communities do you *love* being a part of?

- Which of your communities are lacking boundaries?

- In what groups do you feel loved?

- Which ones are you wanting to invest more in?

My community and the people I surround myself with are *everything* to me! Being known and feeling a sense of belonging—there's nothing like it! When we are in a joyful feeling with a sense of belonging, trust, and safety, our brains enjoy this like nothing else. We need people in our lives who are "God with skin" to us. Period!

9. Exercise. Nothing is better than a great sweat! New neurons grow when we exercise (Smith, 2002).[5] For me, this is another non-negotiable. Strength training and walking are a must! If I can do it, you can do it too!

In closing, I began this chapter telling of my experience of life as someone who lost her way in the busyness of life. I was stopped in my tracks by a faith and health crisis that I'm grateful to have survived. I now share and own my story to hopefully help others see the value in gratitude and optimism.

My faith and spiritual life are not a casual thing for me anymore. Life is like a path. At times it is straight and smooth; at other times it turns and becomes uneven. Today, I stay on the path of faith and well-being through my daily actions because I see the joy in this journey.

Thank you for hearing my story. Take what you like and leave the rest!

I pray that whatever you are facing right now, that these words will be reminders and guideposts in your own self-care and victory as an educator, for God's Kingdom!

My Challenge to You:

Keep a gratitude journal for five weeks with your students and independently. Have them write one to five items for gratitude in a journal or notebook.

Track the results.

Do you feel different even after that short exercise?
What do you observe about the process?
How can you operationalize gratitude into a habit?

Questions for Reflection:

Do you believe your best work is ahead of you?

Why or why not? (Really reflect on this one.)

_____

_____

_____

_____

_____

Who is on your team, helping you sharpen your focus, making you better, giving you accountability in what you do?

_____

_____

_____

Discuss if and how you see the gifts and strength of being grateful.

_____

_____

_____

_____

_____

_____

_____

6

NAVIGATING AND DEBRIEFING TRAUMA

Dr. Jenny Severson

"Trust in the Lord with all your heart and lean not on your own understanding; in all your ways submit to Him and He will make your paths straight."
Proverbs 3:5-6, NIV

THIS CHAPTER WILL ADDRESS THE WORD *trauma,* my understanding of trauma, and then give the educator tools for handling difficult conversations (where trauma many times can begin). The last part of the chapter provides a powerful workplace process that helps leaders navigate traumatic events. This last section is called Trauma Debriefing. Trauma debriefing includes understanding important questions—a must-read for anyone who works with others, whether on a school leadership team, school board, or organization.

The word *trust* is used in the scripture passage noted above. Trust in the Lord with all your heart. Trusting is the ultimate on-the-court experience! *On the court* means real life, not gossip, observations, or armchair views. It means getting out there in the game of life. It takes time, work, and effort. Effort is defined in neuroscience as the "work" our brains do each day . . . one axon and dendrite at a time.

I love the field of neuroscience, and I love this Proverbs 3 passage because it calls into action the hard-wiring of our

71

minds. The passage reminds me how things can change and evolve—how our paths can be made straight. I call upon gratitude and optimism, but I am not naïve to think these practices happen fast or in the twinkling of night one wakes up "paths straight" or "thoughts submitted." It's a process.

As you take clear action each day on the self-care as an educator tool-kit, you will be more grateful. I guarantee it! Please share with me your progress with staff and students as you work the gratitude lists each day. I'd love to hear from you @Severson_J or JennySeverson.com.

This field of mental health—social emotional learning—is important work that is not going away. It is vital to the life of our organizations. Remember, it starts with you. If you have done your own work, and continue to be open, honest, and willing, then and only then, can you help and guide others on their journey.

And so, for today, I want to share with you immediate tools for when you are dealing with others who are facing trauma or navigating their own way back to healing. Most of us need these tools at some point in our careers. For women and school leaders, the next two sections are relevant, actionable strategies for the workplace.

Reflecting back to my personal story, I sought out a Christian counselor. I was shocked to learn what a counselor told me in our first session, as I shared my "fact sheet" with her. She said "Jenny, you've been through trauma."

I said, "Trauma? Really? Nahhh."

Actually, I had no clue. I was so happy to be alive. Literally, I would hug everyone I saw; I would say "Hello" and give high-fives like they were worth $1 million. I was so happy to be back in our hometown around friends and family that I'd known for at least a decade. I was grateful for my work, and that I was able to meet my speaking engagements for the year. Grateful for my hair starting to grow back. Grateful for my husband, children, and insurance. Grateful for the ability to make new choices. Grateful to be back in a community where I wasn't using a GPS to get everywhere, where I knew the roads and the "back way" or "short cuts" to places. These little things matter when you don't have them. Grateful for our new neighbors, our street, our old friends, and the new ones we were meeting each week. Grateful for church family, the birch trees in our backyard, the view from my home office. Grateful for the windows rolled down and the way we were all *breathing a sigh of relief.* Especially me. I started to *breathe* again. I was so shut down before, armored up, but, now, I started to breathe again. I started to move from surviving to thriving.

Now that I am back home and healing, I am still grateful for these two aspects of my life, every day.

So, yes. The gratitude, optimism factors are truly amazing, and being in front of friends, old fellowships, the sense of belonging, to me is extraordinary. I was moving into a new life, a new chapter, which was a huge relief. What I didn't realize is that I would need to process (over the course of an entire eighteen months) this thing called *trauma.* Trauma meaning what happened, what changed, and how I could continue to move forward. I agreed to look at trauma and went to counseling every week.

At first, in my typical fashion, I want to "check off the boxes" (Moved in . . . √. Boxes unpacked . . . √. Paperwork for school/kids . . . √. Dentist and doctor visits . . . √. Counseling . . . √.). However, what I am learning now is about *slowing down*—something I have never truly examined before. The power in slowing down to process is what I offer you today. By talking, writing, reflecting, and teaching others how to do the same, I reinforce my own recovery. Trauma is not about speeding up; it is about slowing down.

It is about actually assessing how one feels and is experiencing, and being more mindful.

As a former building principal and teacher, I wanted to share a format for being a leader and dealing with school situations involving trauma or uncomfortable situations. The ideas listed are strategies I have used in the past. These gems are game-changing and life-changing!

I operate with the definition of *trauma* as "a deeply disturbing or distressing experience" or "physical injury." A traumatic event is an incident that causes physical, emotional, spiritual, or psychological harm. The person experiencing the distressing event might feel threatened, anxious, or frightened as a result. He or she will need support and time to recover from the traumatic event and regain emotional and mental stability.

- Have you ever left a meeting deeply disturbed?
- Have you ever had a distressing experience?
- Have you ever been affected by an incident that caused physical and/or emotional harm?
- How do you approach or avoid these types of situations?

Let's take a look.

As I list these gems that helped me along the way, remember the simplicity in listening to people. The power of listening, saying hello, being greeted with a smile—these are little things that, when you have faced a traumatic situation, your brain picks up. The positive energy, the warm welcome, the statements of gratitude—they really matter! Brains go and thrive where they are loved.

To begin: when you are faced with an uncomfortable conversation:

Sit next to the person, not behind a big desk. Get near

the person and welcome them. Why? A large desk can be seen as a barrier between someone with a title and someone without. Extend your welcome. Be warm and polite, no matter what.

1. Next: Start with a genuine gratitude statement. Acknowledge *anything* going well. For example, "Thanks for being here. I'm grateful you are making the time to connect." Or, "I'm glad that you arrived." Or, "I'm glad we have this chance to communicate, to seek solutions." Or, "I'm grateful that we can be involved in a solution conversation." Or, "Let me first express my gratitude that you are willing to look at a tough topic." Or, "I'm grateful that we have the chance to work together." Get granular on gratitude; it's worth it, every time!

2. Say something you appreciate about the person. Imagine you are a school leader, and a student and parent are involved in your meeting. Begin by saying something that you sincerely appreciate about the student/child. It could be funny or, better yet, connected to something you actually observed. Also, tell the parent what a great job they are doing (I've never met a parent who wasn't second-guessing themselves). There's no manual for parenting per se, and we can all benefit from encouragement on fighting the negativity and shame associated with parenting (*shame* meaning "It's not good enough" or "Who do you think you are?") type messages.

3. Approach the conversation with humility. Say, "I've been very humbled by this situation. I might not know all the right things to do." Maybe even apologize. Why? It puts us on a level playing field. Even if you are working as hard as you can, it lets the other person(s) know that both parties can solve it together and it's not "me vs. you"; rather, it is a "we program not a me program" of solutions. Maybe you apologize for not

having all the answers. So often, in difficult situations, we try to throw all our knowing into it. Those of us who have a faith can invite God's will into the situation. This act of humility and, potentially, apologizing demonstrates a vulnerability that you are asking for help, and that lowers defenses.

4. Before the meeting ends: Ask *them* what they need from you. Create an action plan. Plan to maybe circle back in a few weeks? Even if in the moment you get a request that is unreasonable . . . listen, give it twenty-four hours, pray on it, and, if it makes sense, do it. You will gain trust and confidence. If their suggestion doesn't work, you have additional evidence for your concern. You are showing you are willing to be in the arena trying to find solutions vs. sitting by as an armchair quarterback. Please know, as a teacher and building principal, I've had some crazy parental requests. As long as it doesn't impact other students, safety, or policy, I try my best to honor it.

5. If the conversation has stalled and the student is involved in the meeting, give them time to talk alone. Let the parent and child know that you are going to step out of the room so they can talk in private. This shows them you truly care and respect boundaries.

6. Sometimes a tough conversation turns into a "pep talk." Whether it's a "pep talk" from parent to kid, or teacher to parent, or principal to teacher, honest feedback, or engaged feedback, it takes courage. Be willing to choose courage over comfort! People need to hear the truth in a gentle way! Do whatever it takes to help the conversation move forward. PS: Allow processing time; maybe give Mom and Dad time alone to discuss things before expecting a decision.

7. I'll never forget one of the most powerful string of words spoken to me as I was healing and messing up on these very hard conversations and circling back in the most honest, raw fashion. While in that process, a colleague said to me,

"We don't shoot the wounded here." In that moment, I made a lifelong friend because she met me with empathy instead of sympathy. Do you know the difference between empathy and sympathy? If not, check out Dr. Brené Brown's work! Go online by Googling sympathy/empathy and Dr. Brené Brown. There's a great short video on it.

Remember, in difficult conversations, when we love our neighbor as ourselves, we win. That does not mean we agree with everything in the conversation, but we give space to others to allow them to be heard. Giving space to listen is the good work we are privileged to do. When we forgive, we win— we release ourselves from the bondage of self that so many of us face. When someone listens to you and you feel heard, in the midst of your pain, that action alone is very healing.

Your Turn for Reflection: Life/Workplace Transfer

Which of the strategies did you like best on tough conversations, and why?

_____

_____

_____

_____

What did someone ever do or say for/to you that was extremely helpful in a time you really needed healing and care?

_____

_____

_____

_____

Why did it matter so much?

_____

_____

_____

Let me finish this chapter by addressing a school-wide Trauma Response process.

Why? Well, take a look at it now so you can be equipped in the event something happens. Remember, trauma can involve a bullying incident, a racial comment. If we are honest, we know these types of incidents are happening every day in our schools. How do we reduce these incidents? We do it by teaching gratitude, acting out kindness, and getting in touch with empathy. Take a look with me at this schoolwide process that I describe below. I welcome your feedback JennySeverson.com or @Severson_J as we are on this journey together.

Organization—Trauma Debriefing Plan

This framework is offered with the goal of adding to what you already have in place and potentially grab some new insights. The debriefing plan is specifically for counselors and someone with an outside, objective point of view.

Critical incidents of trauma require processing time. Programs are often written to address the twenty-four to forty-eight hours after the event, when in reality people need about seven to ten days.

Let's talk through the introduction, facts, thoughts, and reactions.

Timing: Give yourself and those involved time to process. For example, do not ask the person whose house just burned down, "Where are you going to live?" What they need first is a hug, water, blanket. Handle first things first. Going too fast causes shame and further upset, and it worsens the hurt and injury.

For schoolwide issues, give yourself, students, and staff some time. You can gather to process as a group or one-on-one depending on the situation. A brief group informational process might have taken place, and distressed individuals might have been supported with one-on-one interventions. Typically, twenty-four to seventy-two hours after, gather the small, homogeneous group.

Trauma Debriefing

Use a structured process that includes the cognitive and affective domains of human experience. The phases are arranged in a specific order to facilitate the transition of the group from the cognitive domain to the affective domain and back to the cognitive again. Although mostly a psycho-educational process, emotions can arise at any time.

Get with a *well-trained* team member to help the group manage some of the emotions.

Phase 1: Intro

In this phase, the team members introduce themselves and describe the process. The goal is for everyone to engage actively in the process. Participation in the discussion is voluntary, and the team keeps the information discussed in the session confidential. A carefully presented introduction sets the tone of the session, anticipates problem areas, and encourages active participation from the group members.

Phase 2: Facts

Only extremely brief overviews of the facts are requested. *Excessive detail is discouraged.* This phase helps the participants to begin talking. It is easier to speak of what happened before they describe how the event impacted them.

The facts phase gets things started. More important parts are yet to come. But giving the group members an opportunity to contribute a small amount to the discussion is enormously important in reducing anxiety and letting the group know that they have control of the discussion. The usual question used to start the fact phase is, "Can you share a brief overview or 'thumbnail sketch' of what happened in the situation from your viewpoint? We are going to go around the room and give everybody an opportunity to speak, if they wish. If you do not wish to say anything you may pass."

Phase 3: Thoughts

The thought phase is a transition from the cognitive domain toward the affective domain. It is easier to speak of what one's thoughts are than to focus immediately on the most painful aspects of the event. The typical question addressed in this phase is, "What was your first thought or your most prominent thought once you realized you were thinking?" Let everyone share.

Your reaction is the heart of any change. Self-care focuses on the impact of the participants. Anger, frustration, sadness, loss, confusion, and other emotions might emerge. The trigger question is, *"What is the very worst thing about this event for you personally?"* The support team listens carefully and gently encourages group members to add something, if they wish. When the group runs out of issues or concerns that they wish to express, the team moves the discussion into the next transition phase, the symptoms phase, which will lead the group from the affective domain toward the cognitive domain.

Debriefing *normalizes the symptoms brought up by participants.* They provide explanations of the participants' reactions and provide stress-management information. Other pertinent topics may be addressed during the teaching phase, as required. For instance, if the session was conducted because of a suicide of a colleague, the topic of suicide should be covered in Phase 1.

In closing, this chapter reveals how we can make our way through traumatic events. We can pick up tools and conversations, and ask for help from each other. We can get with trained professionals who can guide us with important questions and processes.

My Challenge to You:

Watch the Brené Brown clip on empathy vs. sympathy. Tweet/tag your favorite insight @SEVERSON_J

For Further Reflection:

Is there an area of trauma, hurt, resentment, irritability, or upset that you need to let go of? Explain.

_____

_____

_____

_____

Where can you take a small action today toward relieving that hurt?

_____

_____

_____

Whom can you talk to about the event?

_____

Meet Mary Smith

Mary Smith is an accomplished educator, speaker, trainer, author, and leadership development expert. She is the owner and founder of Educational Leadership Consultants, LLC, whose products and services provide fresh insight into the unique challenges facing academia in school districts and organizations worldwide.

Mary is an experienced Ziglar Legacy Certified trainer and coach as well as a Certified DISC Human Behavior Consultant. Drawing on thirty years of educational experience, Mary's mission is to motivate and inspire educators to become the best version of themselves.

Mary hosts a weekly podcast, *An Educator's Legacy*, in which she brings significant players from the world of education to share their stories and provide inspiration to audiences.

A natural connector, Mary engages audiences of any size with her warmth, contagious humor, and relevant expertise. She uses her inexhaustible energy and never-say-never spirit to create dynamite staff-development opportunities for teachers, administrators, and paraprofessional staff.

Mary is a Texas Education Agency (TEA)-approved instructor. Educators can earn their Continuing Professional Education (CPE) credits by taking her classes online at www.ELCSchools.com. Mary is also available to bring her CPE-approved courses to your organization or school district to complete training in-person.

Mary is a published author with titles that include *An Educator's Legacy: Impact and Reflection Journal* and *Reflective Impact Journal: Pursuing Greatness Every Day.*

Mary lives in Houston, Texas, and enjoys speaking at churches across the state. She and her husband, Ronnie, have two children and eight grandchildren.

Meet Mary Smith

Follow Mary Smith
Educational Speaker/Trainer/Coach/Consultant
832-940-9660
msmith@EduLeadConsultants.net
www.EduLeadConsultants.net www.ELCSchools.com
Find her on all social media platforms @eduleadconsultants

7

THE POWER OF PROFESSIONAL JOURNALING

Mary Smith

"*I can do all things through Christ who strengthens me.*"
Philippians 4:13, NKJV

W HAT IF YOU COULD OVERCOME ALMOST EVERY obstacle
that comes your way? What if you could take away
the guilt that comes from the mistakes you've made? Imagine
how free your heart and mind would feel if you could just
release the pain that has a stronghold on you. That is what
this chapter is about—releasing your pain through journaling to grow personally and professionally. Journaling creates
a thought process that is intentional. Journaling is a mindset.
It's about becoming everything God intended for you.

"*I* CAN *do all things through Christ who strengthens me!*
(Philippians 4:13)

I woke up Christmas morning 2015 in Alpine, Texas on
a blow-up mattress in my son's living room, next to my husband's soft snoring. As I lay there, happy to be with my son
and his sweet young family, I realized it was the first Christmas I would spend with him since he had left home some
seven or eight years earlier. As I turned to roll off the bed, I
was hit by a wave of pain around my ribcage so bad it took
my breath away.

I had already been to three different doctors since Thanksgiving trying to figure out what was causing this pain. I was given three different diagnoses with three different rounds of treatment, none of which had worked. I reached down to my side to hold my ribs and noticed there were bumps on my skin. It felt like bubble wrap. I then made my way to the bathroom to look in the mirror.

As I lifted my sleep shirt, I was stunned at the number of dime-, nickel-, and even quarter-sized blisters I saw. They started where my ribcage met in the front and traveled around to my spine in the back. They began just under my right breast and went all the way down to my hip/groin area. They were super sensitive to the touch.

My daughter-in-law is a nurse, so I went into their bedroom and asked her to take a look.

"Could this be shingles?" I asked.

She looked at the spots and said, "Oh, my gosh! I think it is shingles! You know what that means?"

I replied, "Yes. We'll pack and leave now."

There was no way I was going to jeopardize the health of my sweet daughter-in-law, my unborn grandbaby, or my eighteen-month-old grandson.

I woke my husband, showed him my side, and apologized to him, explaining that it was urgent we leave ASAP. I tried to get dressed, but there was no way I was going to put on a bra, so the "girls" got a reprieve. I *never* go out in public without a bra because I am so big-busted that it's actually a health hazard for me.

When we arrived back home in Houston, we went inside to drop off the luggage. I then went back out, got back into the car, and drove myself to the emergency room to be checked out. I lay there in a bed and lifted my shirt for this doctor to see. He stood across the room and wouldn't even come near me. It was official; I had shingles. He acknowledged that my breakout was the worst one he'd ever seen, but there was really not much they could do. He gave me some acyclovir to lessen the outbreak and reduce the amount of time I would blister, then he told me to take it easy.

The pain got worse every day for at least a month, until I was reduced to not getting dressed, not sleeping. Sometimes I was not even able to eat. The pain was so severe.

There were three types of internal pain, and they were actually worse than the blisters. One felt like a round cigarette lighter (like they used to have in cars) slowly drilling its way through my lungs. The second type of pain felt like someone had an ice pick and was using it to stab holes in my lungs. The pain was so severe it literally took my breath away. The third was the dull pain that just lingered. It felt like someone had inserted a softball into my innards between my lungs and ribcage, which made it difficult to catch my breath.

I ended up with a breakout that lasted almost eight months due to a pre-existing condition that had compromised my immune system. The pain was so severe for so long I literally began asking God to just let me die.

It was during this dark time that I first discovered the power of journaling. I was talking to a friend about the amount of pain I was experiencing and that nothing seemed to work. He suggested I put my focus elsewhere. His recommendation was for me to start keeping a gratitude journal.

I had never heard of a gratitude journal, and I wasn't much of a journaling type of girl. It reminded me of writing in a diary, which didn't appeal to me at all. Why on earth would I write down my private thoughts for others to find? It seemed to me that that type of thing could be used against me in a court of law, so writing it down could be detrimental to my future!

I eventually discovered, though, that journaling is different from writing in a diary. Writing in a diary is more of a record of how your day went and your feelings. Writing in a journal is more focused and intentional.

A gratitude journal focuses on seeking ways to be grateful. My friend suggested I look for three to five things a day that I enjoy, appreciate, or admire. During this time in my life, I was laser-focused on the pain, and nothing else. I decided to give it a try because I was desperate.

I began by writing down three things I admired or appreciated, because honestly, I wasn't enjoying anything. It was tough at first—finding three things that I was grateful for when I was miserable! I did manage to find three things at the end of the day I could record.

My first day I was grateful for meat, cheese, and air conditioning. (Hey, you've got to start somewhere!) Each day I then began to look for three things to be grateful for so I wouldn't feel so stuck when I sat down to write them out. At the beginning I was grateful for cheese. . . . a *lot*! I have no idea why, but looking back, I should have invested in a cheese company.

Eventually, my focus shifted from things I appreciated to things I enjoyed, such as phone calls from my children and grandchildren or hearing good news from a friend. I began looking for the positives during the day, and it led to my writing down five things instead of three. Bonus: I noticed that my pain had lessened. It is amazing what your brain can do when you make a conscious choice to do something different.

I ended up incorporating my gratitude journal into my morning Power Hour. For years, I have been getting up an hour earlier than my husband so that I can spend time praying and focusing on my goals. Working on clearly defined goals really begins to change you. As I began to evolve, my journaling evolved as well.

In 2017, I experienced another life-altering event that affected me to my core. I was speaking to a group of IT professionals and talking about how great a job I had done in leaving my personal trash at the door the year I went through a divorce while teaching third grade. After presentations like these, there is usually a line of people waiting to speak to me. This time was no different. One of the people in line was a tall young man who looked somewhat familiar to me, but I couldn't place why I knew him or where from.

When the end of the line came to me and everyone else had left, the young man stepped forward and asked me if my name used to be Mrs. Manning. I replied, "Yes it was," and I asked him if he was in my class.

"Yes, I was."

I looked at his badge and saw that his name was Patrick. I looked at his face again, and realized he had been in my class. I remembered him! He was a nice kid with a very direct personality. He never got into trouble or stepped out of line. He was an all-around great kid.

"Were you in my class the year I got divorced?"

"Yes."

I said, "How do you know?"

He dropped his eyes to the floor and said, "It was the worst year of my academic career."

I managed to ask him, "How could you tell?"

His reply, "You were just so angry."

I was devastated in hearing this. I looked at him and apologized for my anger. I explained it wasn't directed at him or the other students. I also told him I had no idea I had done that. He accepted my apology and said he now understood, although he hadn't understood back then.

Patrick left, and I gathered the rest of my things and headed out to my car, where I ugly-cried for the next ten minutes before I could even begin the drive home. Of course, I thought things like . . .

- If I ruined his year, then I probably ruined everyone's year, because if he noticed my anger, chances are everyone noticed.

- To how many kids did I actually give their worst year, because the emotions that accompany divorce or any other trauma don't magically disappear in a year or less?

- And finally (the ever dramatic) I wonder if I was a decent teacher at all? Or did I just make kids miserable for all eighteen years I was in the classroom?

As I reflected on this feedback, I realized if I had not been so obsessed with the pain or stress of divorce or the constant fear that we would soon be homeless, I might have been able to give him (and me and my children) a better year.

Then it hit me! What if I had known about a gratitude journal at the time I was going through divorce? What if I had realized that by focusing on something positive, the negativity (and in my case, anger) could have been reduced?

We are educators, but we are also humans, who experience various traumas. Many times we don't have the luxury of taking a year off to get through the hurt. We have to go to work and tough it out. If I had been able to record some positives that were happening throughout the day, maybe I would not have been so angry.

Which brings me to 2019, which is when I decided to write a journal for educators. Every single one of us will face a low point in life in one way or another. It might be a personal life-threatening illness, the loss of a loved one, the ending of a marriage, or the experience of being abused. We have to have something positive to focus on because the pain, stress, grief, or anxiety can be overwhelming and detrimental to self and careers.

You might not have any say in what life throws at you, but you definitely have a choice in how you respond. I get to choose how I handle any stressful situation I find myself in or information that I receive. I had the ability to choose to let the information from my student Patrick continue to guilt me out for the rest of my life or create something productive from the situation that might possibly help others. I chose the latter and wrote *An Educator's Legacy, Impact and Reflection Journal.*

Giving yourself the ability to focus on something positive that takes place each day actually releases dopamine in your brain and elevates your mood. It allows you to see the difference you are making in your classroom, whether it is making little Johnny smile, the satisfaction that everyone in class has scored well on their science test, or doing something nice for another person who is suffering. It doesn't matter. We look for the good.

I found an article dated August 17, 2017, at QZ.com, entitled "I Spent Years Discovering the Simple Tactics Gurus like Oprah, Einstein, and Buffet Used to Become Successful—Here They Are," by Michael Simmons[1], in which he identified some famous people who had kept journals. They include Ben Franklin, Peter Drucker, and Leonardo da Vinci.

Also, Steve Jobs stood at the mirror each day and asked, "If today were the last day of my life, would I want to do what I am about to do?" Arianna Huffington counts her blessings each morning, and Oprah Winfrey keeps a gratitude journal, listing five things she is grateful for every day.

In recent years there have been many articles on the

power of professional journaling. The authors of these articles cite things such as clarity in both patterns of behavior and setting the true goals you would like to achieve. They talk about keeping a running record of good ideas, a safe place to vent, and a way to keep up with compliments you receive throughout the day.

There are health benefits as well. Research shows that journaling reduces stress, improves memory function, invokes mindfulness, and strengthens your immune system. Some research is showing it might help regulate emotions as well.

Many authors suggest how strong the practice of reflective journaling can be. Looking at a situation, challenge, or obstacle, and reflecting on not only what led to the event but also what could have been done differently or what other outcomes could have been possible will many times lead to a solution.

As reported by Kimberly D. Tanner in "Promoting Student Metacognition" (*The American Society for Cell Biology*)[2], reflective journals were proven to increase student achievement and were a key in metacognitive performance. There are hundreds of other research papers citing how writing improves metacognitive thinking. If writing is proven to be a key performance indicator for students, we know it will work for us, too.

Have you ever had a conundrum that was bothering you and it didn't seem to have a favorable solution? Sometimes the simple act of putting it on paper will spark the creative fire needed to resolve the matter.

One year I had a principal at a school where I taught and with whom I did *not* get along. She was snobby, ranked people according to their job, and wouldn't speak when spoken to when she was walking down the hall. One day I asked her why she didn't respond when I said hello to her in passing. Her reply, "I don't have time to talk to everyone who speaks to me. I have important things on my mind."

The truth is, I should have never called out that principal, but I did because it just really bothered me that she wasn't friendly enough to acknowledge a hello. After I called her out that day, she started writing me up for every single move I made, no matter how dumb—such as walking through the wrong door or passing out papers in class. She found something to write me up about every single day for five solid years. One thing is for sure—she was persistent.

At the end of each year, I would think I needed to get another job or transfer buildings or do something else, because she was making my life miserable. If I had known about journaling back then, I could have solved some of the obvious problems like how I could better navigate the school environment the principal had created. Or, I could have reflected on how I wanted my relationship with her to develop. I did spend a lot of time thinking about those things, but there is a power to the written word that I was missing. Seeing it on paper and being able to reflect, redirect, and get those Aha! moments would have helped tremendously.

We as educators, often find ourselves in this situation. We have Wow! moments, Yikes! moments, professional questions we ponder, fears we need to tackle, and goals we want to accomplish. In early 2020, Pete Hall, Alisa Simeral, and I published *Reflective Impact Journal: Pursuing Greatness Every Day*[3] in an effort to provide educators the ability to become the greatest professional versions of themselves possible. It is a great tool that will lead you to your greatness!

Fortunately for me, life outside of school was better than it was at school. I was working three jobs trying to put food on the table *and* pay the rent. I had shed 160 pounds in the form of Ron No. 1—the prototype, and I had personally lost weight of my own and had begun dating again. I was even dating Ron No. 2, the upgraded version that I would eventually marry. (Not the same Ron; two completely different men!) Plus, my kids were becoming happy children. . . . no more fear in our home!

While my life at school stunk out loud, my personal life was becoming more manageable. I was focused on student achievement in hopes it would help my principal like me more, but it didn't. She and I just didn't get along.

I made a decision to tough it out, though. I knew I needed to stay right where I was for my kids' sake. They had already been through so much with the divorce, and they needed the stability of the school and their friends. I suffered through five years of her giving me heck, only to have my last year with her turn out to be an amazing year of being able to do no wrong. Go figure!

I followed a process that is very similar to reflective journaling, but I didn't write it down because I wasn't aware of journaling at the time. However, I *did* reflect on the situations in which I kept finding myself. I just talked to myself a lot, making people think I truly was crazy! The power in writing it down is that it keeps the focus on the problem and the "squirrel" moments are few and far between!

Here's the process:

1. Write down the situation.

2. Reflect on what led up to the situation. Were there triggers that generated the outcome produced?

3. Identify what you can change and what you have no control over. Don't spend any time on the things you have no control over, but focus on the things you can work on.

4. Record *all* the possible outcomes that could have occurred, positive, negative, or neutral.

5. Identify the outcome you would like, and choose an action or strategy that you can implement, eliminate, or alter that would produce a more favorable outcome.

My Challenge to You:

Do some reflective journaling. It takes only a few minutes a day. Ask yourself some questions that will help you grow in whatever area in which you want to grow. We all strive to be the best version of ourselves we can be, but that cannot occur unless we are willing to stretch out of our comfort zone. If you want to see massive growth, get comfortable with being uncomfortable.

Here's a sample to get you started:

1. What did I learn from this process?

2. Did I receive any feedback on my work today? If so, what was it and how can I use it?

3. What can I do to stretch myself to help me grow in the area in which I would like to further develop?

4. What progress did I make today? What progress did my students make today?

5. What can I do to avoid repeating my mistakes?

6. What do I like most/least about my job, classroom climate, student management system, campus, etc.?

7. How can I improve the systems that are already in place?

8. How can I change to attain what is required for me to feel more successful in what I am trying to achieve?

9. What can I do to be happier in my work, home, personal, or spiritual life?

10. What can I do to be a better teacher/assistant principal/principal/district leader/ superintendent?

11. What legacy am I creating with those around me?

12. What positive step can I take to increase my likelihood of success on _____ ?

If you are walking through a storm of life right now and need a journal to help you focus on the positives, or if you just want to focus on the positives, order *An Educator's Legacy, Impact and Reflection Journal*, at www.EduLeadConsultants.net/shop. If you would like the *Reflective Impact Journal: Pursuing Greatness Every Day*, you can pick it up at https://store.mcrel.org/

Otherwise, grab a notebook, pad of paper, or napkin, and start writing!

8
UNDERSTANDING PERSONALITY PATTERNS

Mary Smith

"Do everything without grumbling or arguing."
Philippians 2:14

WHAT IF COMMUNICATION ERRORS WERE NONEXISTENT? What if you could speak to people in such a way that they want to hear what you have to say and they want to engage in an actual conversation with you—without their phone?

One day I was in a large department store shopping and found myself in the men's department. I *love* shopping in the men's department; you usually run into some pretty good-looking men there! I noticed they had men's slacks on sale, so I called my husband and asked him one question: Do you need dress pants for work?

This was his response: "I have a brown pair, a black pair, a tight pair of navy-blue pants," and then he went on and on and on listing every pair of pants he has in his closet. However, he did not answer my question.

When he took a breath, I jumped in again with, "Do you need dress pants for work?"

His response: "I told you, I have a brown pair, a couple of pairs of tight pants, a black pair . . . "

I cut him off and asked once more: "Do you need dress pants for work? It's a yes or no question."

His response was the same, "I have a brown pair, a black pair. Some are too tight . . . "

At that point I said, "Never mind. You have yet to answer my question, and I've asked it three times. I wouldn't pick up pants for you if they were giving them away!" and I hung up the phone.

Have you ever had a conversation like that—where it seems like you are communicating with an alien? The above conversation frustrated me so much that I contemplated stepping in front of a bus just so I would not have to hear what was in his wardrobe anymore! I am just kidding about the bus bit. I am more of a push-him-in-front-of-the-bus kind of girl.

We have all experienced conversations that have gone haywire or been completely misconstrued. After all, we know what we are thinking and trying to say; why can't people understand us?

Case in point:

When I was in the classroom, I had a partner who was super sweet and an absolutely phenomenal teacher. She was actually named teacher of the year several times.

Our first year as partners teaching third grade, she taught language arts and I taught math and science. Her students were constantly doing plays, read-alouds, and speeches. Honestly, it looked like constant chaos in her room, but her kids were always on task doing something they loved that accelerated their learning by leaps and bounds. I guess they thought I needed a little softening up, so they partnered me with her. I could tell when I met her that she was scared to death of me.

One day early in the year, my kids were taking a quiz but having trouble concentrating because of all the noise coming from her room. We were an open-concept school, separated only by two cabinets. While my students couldn't see everything going on, they could see enough to be super distracted by all the fun happening next door. I stuck my head around the corner and simply said, "Can y'all keep it down over here? My kids are trying to take a test."

She looked up at me, told her kids to be quiet, and burst into tears. Not just eyes welling up, but crying. Her kids started rallying around her because she was crying, and I just stood there. I couldn't figure out what the heck was going on.

All I did was ask them to keep it down, and now she's crying like a baby and everyone hates me.

Each person has personality patterns that are intrinsically wired into them. Some personalities are strong, bold, and somewhat loud. Others are more reserved, soft-spoken, and sweet. Learning about the personality styles of others and how to best communicate with them will take your relationships to the next level.

The DISC Model of Human Behavior is based on research first conducted by William Moulton Marston (1893-1947). In 1928, Marston published the book *Emotions of Normal People*, in which he theorized there are four basic personality pattern styles.

Most people will identify with a primary style; however, we are all a unique blend of each of the letters. Marston never created an assessment to determine a person's personality style, he simply identified the four styles. Since, many people have interpreted his research to be very effective in communication techniques. It is the most widely used personality model in the world.

Here is the model:
D stands for **D**ominant
I stands for **I**nspiring
S stands for **S**upportive
C stands for **C**autious

When working within the DISC Model of Human Behavior, it is important for you to understand *your* strongest personality pattern and your unique blend. In addition to the four personality patterns listed above, there are actually forty-one unique blends that make each of us different. *Forty-one!*

Go online now and take your free test here:

https://disc.elcschools.com/quiz

Now that you have taken your personality profile assessment, let's dive into what that means.

Full Disclosure: I am a high-D, high-I personality style. That means I like to get things done and have fun! What does your personality style say about you?

Outgoing vs. Reserved Personality Styles

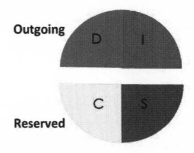

In the DISC Model of Human Behavior, the D and the I have outgoing personality traits. They like to talk and do not mind being the center of attention. Outgoing personality types usually have bigger, bolder personality styles and never meet a stranger.

Reserved personality styles, the C and the S, are shy and do not feel the need to have such a large presence in a room. They don't mind working behind the scenes to support others.

Task-Oriented vs. People-Oriented Personality Styles

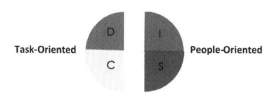

Viewed another way, you can look at the styles based on orientation. Typically, the D and the C personality styles are more task-oriented. Task-oriented people like checking off their to-do list. These people will always get the job done.

I and S personality styles are more people-oriented. People-oriented people like to talk. They love to socialize and be around others. They not only like being around others, but they are really good at building strong relationships.

Let's look at each of the personality style letters. We will start with D and work our way to C.

Strong-D Personality Style

The D stands for Dominant. There's a reason the D is known as a dominant personality type: they are very direct in their communication style. They say what they mean and they mean what they say.

- They are decisive. Nothing makes them crazier than someone who can't make a decision. They would rather make the wrong decision than make no decision. They also like a quick decision. D's do not like being told what to do, but they do love to be given choices.

- They are doers. They naturally do whatever it takes to get the job done. If you need new life breathed into a project, put a D in the mix and watch what happens.

- They are driven. They have an internal motivation that keeps their motor running at a hundred miles per hour . . . all the time. Many times, they'll wake up in the middle of the night thinking about all the things they need to do, and then have difficulty turning off their mind to get back to sleep. They're like the Energizer bunny! (This is me!)

- Often, they can also be seen as defiant. I can tell you that, as a high-D personality type, I am not defiant. It's just that my way is better than your way, so I'm going to do it my way regardless of what you say!

Only about 10 percent of the population has a strong D personality style. For that we should all be truly thankful. Imagine a world full of strong D personalities bulldozing their way through life!

Strong I Personality Style

I stands for Inspiring. These people like to influence others. They love to sway people to their way of thinking. These people are the people that are in it for the fun, and sometimes that means you end up in trouble. If you're going to end up in trouble, the person to be in trouble with would be an I, because you will have fun! Why not make the best of every situation!

- They are inclusive. They never meet a stranger and will include almost anyone in their party. I personality traits typically don't discriminate. They love having lots of people around.

- They are interesting. They get out and experience life, so they have many interesting stories to tell. I had a roommate in college once who was so high-I-oriented that she would actually leave the dorm room and just walk around campus so she could talk to people. I never saw her sitting in our room studying by herself, but she was always part of a study group!

- They are interchangeable. They have a best friend at home; they have a different best friend at school; they have another best friend at soccer practice; they have a different best friend at church; they have a best friend everywhere they go! They love people and have a million best friends!

- I personality types can sometimes be perceived as irresponsible. Some people think they are more interested in having fun than in adulting.

About 25-30 percent of the population has a strong I personality style. Thankfully, about one-fourth to one-third of the people on our planet strive to make life fun! They bring us laughter and good times!

Strong S Personality Style

S stands for Supportive. When I think of the S personality type, I think *sweet*. These people are just plain sweet. They enjoy friendly environments that are harmonious. They love it when everyone can be in the same room together and be nice and kind to each other. Conflict and tension make them nervous and anxious.

- They are sincere. When they say something, and it's usually something sweet, they are being very sincere. They are also very agreeable. An S personality type can be such a people pleaser that they very seldom say the word *no*.

- Many times they are shy. Their personality type is more reserved and they don't feel the need to be the center of attention. They are content to be in the shadows supporting those around them or those who need to be the center of attention.

- They are steady. By that, I mean they have a slower pace than a D or an I, but it's because they are more reserved and steadier in their actions and words.

- However, some people think they are suckers because they don't like to disappoint others, and they are so agreeable. They aren't suckers, but they are supportive and noncombative.

The S personality type is the largest percentage of the population, numbering 30-35 percent. I am so thankful that most of the planet consists of sweet people. If we didn't have these sweet people helping us to stay calm and get along, there would be so much more conflict in the world.

Strong C Personality Style

C stands for Cautious. C personality types are compliant. They love rules, procedures, and systems. They help define our world and give us boundaries.

- They are also competent. Cs' favorite characteristic about themselves is their competence and being correct. They love facts, figures, research, and proof. Don't tell them to change a system, procedure, or rule, unless you have some valid proof to follow it up, and it had better make sense to them as well. If you do need to change something, make sure you give them plenty of notice, like three to four years.

- They are conscientious. They really work hard to make sure they are doing a great job. They thrive on being the best at what they do and they are very detail-oriented.

- C personality types are change resistant. They have used their super-smart, analytical mind to develop procedures and systems that are super-efficient and high functioning. They don't need someone coming along to reinvent the wheel that is already perfectly balanced.

- However, the C personality can be perceived as cold because they are difficult to read. They don't display much emotion and people have a difficult time reading them.

C personality styles make up about 20-25 percent of the population! They allow us to have order, boundaries, and control over ourselves and our environment.

Communicating Between Personality Styles

When communicating, different personality styles prefer different communication styles.

If you are communicating to a D personality style, you want to be direct and quick. (Notice I only have one sentence for this style—that's all we need!)

When communicating to an I personality style, make sure you ask about their family, friends, and interests. You'll want to speak at a faster pace because they are typically easily distracted. People who talk too slow will have difficulty talking to an I because the I's mind moves quickly, and slow talk is boring to them.

When communicating to an S personality style, make sure you slow your pace so you don't scare them. Be friendly, and allow them time to make decisions. They are uncomfortable having to make decisions too quickly.

When communicating to a C personality style, make sure you are speaking at a slower pace (due to their reserved personality style), and come prepared by knowing your facts, figures, research, etc. Above all, give them time to adjust to any changes you would like to make. They are resistant to change, so give them time to process any changes that need to be made, and make sure you have a good reason for making the changes.

Remember the story I told you about at the beginning with my partner teacher? Turns out, she was a high-S personality type. She did not like confrontation and would do anything to keep the peace, be supportive, and be agreeable. High-D and high-S personality styles are polar opposites, as are high-I and high-C personality styles.

I am a high-D, high-I personality style. I am very direct in my communication style. My partner teacher I mentioned earlier perceived my asking her to keep it down as the equivalent to telling her I don't really like her and she's not doing a very good job. On top of that, I said it in front of all her kids. There were three things I learned that day.

1. I needed to watch *what* I said to her.
2. I needed to watch *how* to say it.
3. I needed to say it *in private*.

My Challenge to You:

Look at your personality style and take into consideration the personality styles of those with whom you interact on a daily basis. Are you a high-I personality style partnered with a C personality style? If so, your partner isn't going to appreciate your socialization as much as you would think. They would prefer that you say what you need, give them proof, research, facts, or figures to support your request, and then allow them time to think about your request. They don't like to make snap decisions and need time to process things.

Think about some of the people you work with. Can you identify them as a D, I, S, or C personality style? Are they strong, bold, and to the point? They are most likely a D. Are they always talking about their friends, family, or having fun? They are probably an I. Are they great listeners and love to be supportive of others? They might be an S. Are they competent and confident in all they do? Chances are they are a C. Just knowing what the personality styles are of the people you work with empowers you to speak to them with confidence in a way that you know will be heard.

What if we communicated with students in our classrooms based on their personality styles? Did you know high-I's spend more time in the office than any other personality style? It's because they just want to talk and have fun. Take that into account when planning partner or group work so as to allow the I personality time to socialize while they do their work.

Imagine a behavior-management system based on knowing the primary personality styles of your students and speaking to those styles when planning lessons and activities instead of a continuum of consequences.

As you interact with others, consider their strongest personality style. How would you use the information you've learned about your own dominant personality style and the four personality profiles to communicate more effectively with them?

The best solution: Train your staff on how to use the DISC personality profile to improve communication between staff and students.

Journal Prompts:

What is the dominant personality pattern you see in your partner, child/ren or person with whom you work most closely?

What communication techniques can you use with them to build an even stronger relationship of trust and respect?

Looking at your own personality style, how can you respectfully communicate with them while maintaining your own integrity?

How has your awareness of your own personality style changed the way you communicate with those to whom you are closest?

Meet Tami West, PhD

Known as "the Funny Motivational Speaker," **Dr. Tami West** uses her renowned, entertaining, and compelling style to shine a refreshingly new light on how to transform your life and discover solutions to life's challenges. For more than fifteen years, Tami has been equipping people to live their best lives. Her passion stems from a lifelong battle with an anxiety disorder that has uniquely equipped her to teach, encourage, and motivate others.

Owner of a bachelor's degree in biology and a master's in education, Tami has worked in a variety of medical settings and has served as a public school teacher. In 2013, she received her PhD in human development and continued her career as the dynamic motivational speaker, trainer, and author she is today.

As a respected and in-demand speaker, Dr. West has spoken in forty-eight states across the US, as well as in the United Kingdom, Australia, and New Zealand. In any given year, Tami speaks to groups with audiences consisting of anywhere from a hundred to three thousand people.

Tami has a knack for being able to communicate with a wide diversity of clientele ranging from Danbury Federal Prison inmates (the setting of the Netflix series *Orange Is the New Black*) to public school teachers to senior management at the Social Security Administration.

Dr. West is the author of several successful publications including two books: *The Stress Club: Stop Participating, Take Your Power Back, and Start Living Your Own Life;* and *Life Without the Monsters.* She also hosts a weekly podcast, *Consider Yourself Hugged.*

Tami enjoys reading historical fiction, traveling with her husband and kids, and watching *The Big Bang Theory.*

Meet Tami West, PhD

Follow Tami West, PhD
tamiwest.com
tamiwest@tamiwest.com
Twitter @TamiWest
Facebook: www.facebook.com/TamiWestSeminars
LinkedIn: www.linkedin.com/in/tamiwest/

9
ANXIETY: FINDING REST FOR YOUR SOUL

Dr. Tami West

"Come to Me, all you who labor and are heavy laden, and I will give you rest. Take My yoke upon you and learn from Me, for I am gentle and lowly in heart, and you will find rest for your souls. For My yoke is easy and My burden is light."
Matthew 11:28-30

WHAT IF INSTEAD OF YOUR ANXIETY CONTROLLING you, you controlled it?

I jumped in the car and sped off. I had no idea where I was going. No plan. I just knew that I could *not* drive to that building. I could *not* face that classroom. I could *not* get in front of those students. Honestly, I don't remember if I told my husband or not. He was home with our own three children, ages two, four, and six. I don't recall what I was thinking. Maybe I envisioned freezing in front of them. A war scene from *Game of Thrones*? Being eaten by *The Walking Dead*? A rumble from *West Side Story*? There was no evidence of any of that. It wasn't logical.

I remember thinking I didn't know how I got into this place. I remember thinking, *Is this going to be my life now? Was my mental hospital stay just the beginning of a life of panic?*

At some point I felt the gradual calm that came with the medication I took before I left—Klonopin, the only drug that brought me down "off the ledge." My mind settled. My thoughts slowed. I knew I wasn't in danger. I returned home, went to school, and went about my life.

Sometime in January 1996

And . . . I survived.

Although many factors contributed to that day in the car and the mental hospital stay, one experience precipitated this stage of my life—my student teaching experience.

It was the spring of 1992. I was almost finished with my required teacher-certification courses and was ready to do my student teaching. I was excited, scared, worried—all probably normal emotions. Not only was I getting ready to student teach fulltime for nine weeks, I was working a part-time job. I was pregnant, had to care for my other two small children, and I was taking my final required class. I could do it. After all, *Perfectionist* was my middle name.

I began my student-teaching experience with a woman whom I had observed previously. The school was close to home, and she was so inviting. "Oh, come student teach with me!" she said. "It'll be great!" she said. It was not.

About two weeks into the semester, my university teacher came for a visit. To my surprise, the teacher with whom I was working told my university teacher I didn't belong in teaching and that I had no initiative. I couldn't believe what she was saying. My supervisor thought it best to remove me from the situation and place me in another school. What I wanted to do was to crawl under a rock. But what would people think if I didn't do it?

Even though I was feeling inadequate, my supervisor

found another teacher who agreed to work with me, and I arrived for my first day. The new teacher's comforting words were, "I can't babysit you! If you can do this, fine, but I don't have a lot of time. I'm only doing this as a favor to a friend!" Each day I would come in, and she and the other coaches would be laughing and talking, with not even a *hello* to me.

It was as if life was a video on repeat.

My supervisor again came for a visit at this second school, and the same scenario played out. I was devastated. That night I went home and experienced the beginning of what would be a difficult battle with panic attacks, reminiscent of attacks I had had as a child, but I had made up my mind that she wasn't going to get to me—I could do it! I marched back in there the next day scared out of my skin. It was too much. I was pregnant and began experiencing pre-term labor. I was hospitalized. Physically, I could have gone back several days later, but mentally I simply could not make myself. I felt defeated.

I went through a difficult time and felt like a failure. It didn't matter what anyone said. I knew I had failed and that I would never be the same again. After my son was born, things became somewhat normal again. When he was nine months old, I decided to try again. It was difficult, but I did it—I accepted a student-teaching position and finished it.

The time came to apply for a teaching job. A nearby county had an opening for a physical science teacher, and I was offered the position. School was starting in about a week, and each night I would sit down to write lesson plans so I would be prepared in advance. My mind wouldn't let me. It had other plans. I obsessed and worried, obsessed and worried, obsessed and worried, etc., etc., etc. I would play little videos in my head of terrible things that might happen. I was jealous of everyone else who could just go to work—*normal* people!

I showed up on the administrative day for teachers, and I even came back for the first day with students. Things went fine those first two days. That is the frustrating thing about worry and anxiety: most of our "what-if's" *never* happen! But that didn't matter. The minute I left the school building, my mind went crazy, and I went right back to worrying. I could not see things as they really were. I was so distraught that I could not go return to that building another day. I really mean *could not*. I made my family call to say I had become ill and would not be able to return.

I was officially a failure, and I had a very difficult time functioning for several weeks. I was embarrassed and constantly worried about what everyone must think of me. Maybe the things those teachers had said were true. Time passed, and I finally snapped out of it. I decided to try again. This time I applied to a different county, where no one knew me. I was offered the position, but this time the anxiety was even worse. Again, my family had to make the phone call with excuses.

I don't believe I was ever truly suicidal, but I could not imagine living the rest of my life that way. I was completely broken, the lowest I had ever been in my life. How could I ever face my family and friends again? What would they think of me? How could anyone ever see me the same way again after what I'd done? All of these gross exaggerations kept playing in my mind. In August 1995, my medical doctor decided it was time to admit me to the hospital. It had been weeks since the job incident, and I could barely leave my bedroom, take care of my children or the house, eat, or drink.

After my release I continued with medication and counseling. I reapplied for a position at the second school I had tried before, and they hired me. They did not know the circumstances surrounding my hospitalization, only that I was ill. The first year or two were rough, but I made it! I would teach a total of ten years before leaving to write my first book and dive into the world of motivational speaking.

I learned a great deal from my years as a teacher experiencing anxiety. Since leaving public education in 2005, I have dedicated my professional life to helping others fight the battle of worry and anxiety. I have prayed and read. I have learned and have grown. I am not perfect by any means, but I know the five strategies you are about to read will put you on the path to thriving.

1. Determine if you are experiencing Anxiety or an Anxiety Disorder.

As you read my story, hopefully you were thinking, *Well, I'm not that bad! I was never in the mental hospital!* The first step to managing your worry is to determine where you are on the anxiety spectrum. We all have anxiety from time to time. The American Psychological Association defines it as "an emotion characterized by feelings of tension, worried thoughts, and physical changes like increased blood pressure." It becomes a disorder when it interferes with your life.

This must be the first step in controlling anxiety: determining if it is an occasional, unwanted emotion, or whether it is a disorder requiring treatment

What can you do?

The Anxiety and Depression Association of America has a screening tool for Generalized Anxiety Disorder. The first question is "Do you experience excessive worry?" You can find the tool at https://adaa.org/screening-generalized-anxiety-disorder-gad

There are many other organizations that can help. Start by reaching out to one.

If you believe you're dealing with occasional anxiety and not a disorder, consider the way you talk to yourself about your anxiety. Oftentimes, I would want to be *normal*. I would be angry at myself for my worries. I would sometimes feel like I would feel anxious forever or that it was more than I could bear. In reality, the feeling was temporary; often it was the same feeling most others felt, and we *can* bear it! Talk to yourself that way. :)

2. Think, think, and think some more!

For years I have been telling a shortened version of the student teaching and hospitalization experience. I would always say, "My hospitalization was related to my student teaching and the way the supervising teachers treated me," which is completely true. But it wasn't until I went back to school for my PhD that I did more self-reflection. Part of my anxiety came before those teachers entered my life: I deeply desired to remain home with my three children. The nurses even wrote in my hospital admission notes: "Her husband is very supportive and will help take care of the children." That only made it worse. But no one heard it.

I believe many of you *know* things deep down that you are sometimes afraid to say. All I could hear with all of these offers to help (the grandparents offered to help, too), was "Take the job, take the job, take the job!!" And I wasn't ready to take the job. Maybe I would have been fine working another job just for the income, one that wasn't such high pressure at a time when my energy needed to go to my children. I believe if you really take time to stop and think why you are worrying, something new will be revealed.

What can you do?

Get in touch with unspoken, maybe even unrecognized, thoughts. If you struggle with anxiety at all, you probably have moments every day when you feel anxious. Whenever you feel a flare-up during your day, pause for a moment (truly, a minute should do it), and then think about all of the following statements and address each by filling in the blank after each:

- This made me anxious:

  _____

  _____

- Here's something I haven't verbalized:

  _____

  _____

- Here's why I haven't (the risk, e.g. maybe you're afraid that speaking up will make you look weak):

  _____

  _____

- I'm willing/not willing (circle one) to address the issue at this time.

  _____

  _____

Over time, you might discover many things you didn't know about yourself when it comes to issues that cause you anxiety, whether it be relationships with students and/or adults, lesson planning, grading, balancing work and home, and more.

3. Identify yourself positively.

A few years ago I was doing a session on stress with a group of teachers. We were talking about how we identify ourselves, and I was talking about a phenomenon I'd seen where people at conferences have ribbons on their badges. These ribbons say things such as "First-time Attendee," "Chapter President," "Speaker," etc. Some conferences have fundraisers where you pay a dollar for a ribbon. I began to notice some of these ribbons: "OCD," "Perfectionist," and "Stressed." Of course, they were intended to be funny, but how we identify ourselves matters.

At the end of the session, a sweet young teacher came to me and said, "For a long time I've said 'Oh this is the worst! Worst group of students! Worst curriculum! Worst day!' My co-teachers bought me this ribbon that says, 'The Worst,' and we all laughed. I wear it on my ID badge every day." I get it. She laughed. They laughed. They bonded over it. But let's think on that at a deeper level. She was walking around every day with a badge that said "The Worst." I say *was* walking around because, thank God, she gave that badge to me at the end of the session. "No more!" she said.

So many times, you might identify yourself in ways that are destructive simply because you have always done it. "Oh, I'm just a worrywart that's just me! I get mad easily—everybody knows that's just who I am! I have high expectations—I'm a perfectionist, that's me!"

Put some thought into uplifting ways to identify yourself. Maybe it's I am *dedicated, strong, caring, bold, confident.*

What to do:

a. Make a list of ways you've described yourself as a woman and teacher, and put a + or – next to it.

Next to the negative descriptions (the - marks), choose new identities. I've created a list for you to download. Just go to https://www.tamiwest.com/free-downloads and find "My Identity Choices."

_____

_____

_____

_____

_____

_____

_____

This will be a work in progress. Now, during the school day and at home, begin speaking your new identity into being!

4. Adopt a new view on stress.

Disclaimer: What I talk about here is what I call _normal daily life_: going to school, teaching, lesson planning, taking care of family, making dinner, paying bills, shuttling kids around, volunteering, etc. If you are going through trauma, I am not talking specifically to you, although this can help! I encourage you to also visit traumasurvivorsnetwork.org for a list of helpful resources.

This topic is difficult to condense—I wrote an entire book on it (_The Stress Club_) based on my 2013 dissertation.

I hope you will check that out! There were two reasons I decided to study women and stress. First, I realized that despite all of this stress advice, statistics continue to worsen for women. And second, I noticed something interesting about women's conversations. It appeared, on a surface level at least, that they were trying to compete for the title of Most Stressed.

The first thing I did in my study was to look at messages that come to us every day about stress. By messages I mean TV commercials, magazine ads, news stories, and Internet articles. Many of them depict women as being stressed out. Now you might be thinking, *Well, I AM stressed out! Stay with me*. For example, I found a magazine ad for makeup that said, "We all have to do ten things at once. Perfectly." Another is for miniblinds. A woman says, "I go a million miles a minute so I conserve energy wherever I can."

Begin paying attention. You will see ads that try to sell you products because life is bad. "Life is busy." "We aren't supposed to rest." "We shouldn't sleep." "We should run from sunup to sundown." "We should be stressed all the time." Here is the problem:

We begin to get our very identities in stress.

Who would I be if I gave that up? I wanted to understand this apparent link between identity and stress, so I went straight to the sources. I had conversations with women who self-identified as stressed-out. The most powerful statement of all of the hours of interviews with thirty women, mostly teachers, was this:

It's like you're not validated if your suffering is not the same.

When I advocate a new view on stress, this is what I mean: Do not embrace it. Refuse it. Reject it. Speak about it differently. I know it's hard. If you are sitting in a team meeting or the faculty lounge and everyone is saying how stressed they are and you say you rested last night, you might hear something like, "Wow must be nice! Wish I could do that! You must not have a lot going on!"

You might feel left out of the stress club. You might feel like you're being accused of being irresponsible.

What to do

This is the hardest thing I will ask you to do in either of my two chapters in this book.

a. Consider losing the word *stress* and adopting other words. When we lump everything under the word *stress*, we lose our power. We cease being able to address issues that are bothering us. Identify how you feel and use those words instead. Are you *anxious, angry, frustrated, overwhelmed, tired, sad*? . . . In the world of teaching where you sometimes feel powerless, take your power back by focusing on what you can control.

b. Talk differently to your friends. For example, someone might say to you, "Wow, must be nice—you went to the movies last night. I graded till midnight!" It's tempting to jump in and justify why you were able to go. *Resist!* Simply say something like, "It was a wonderful night."

Over time, you will train yourself to reject the notion that life should never be good, and you will forfeit your membership in the stress club!

5. Guard and use your senses wisely.

I remember my first year of teaching, at the height of my anxiety, one of those inspirational teacher movies came out: *Mr. Holland's Opus.* My teacher friends *raved* about it! Me? All I could think was, *Ahhh, why can't I be like that?? I'm an awful teacher, so bad!* So let's talk about all five of your senses:

What to do:
a. **Your eyes:** Be very cautious about what your eyes see! There are so many events you have no control over. Maybe you see a fight in the hallway. You didn't ask for it, yet there it is. That fight is in your mind all day, increasing your anxiety. So why would you let in images that hurt you on purpose? I did not watch those teacher movies, like *Mr. Holland's Opus*, at all while I was teaching. Maybe others were motivated by them, but for me it caused painful comparisons. Watch things that lift you up!

b. **Your ears:** Again, there are so many sounds you didn't ask to hear—a student crying. Your anxiety heightens. So why let damaging sounds in? This includes gossip, negativity, and music that increases your angst. Be cautious. Listen to sounds that lift you up!

c. **Your mouth:** Be aware of foods that heighten your anxiety, and don't use them! Caffeine, maybe? And also put things in your mouth that make you happy, without over-indulging. Have some of that special chocolate that puts a pep in your step.

d. **Your skin:** Have special things in your classroom—a blanket you drape over your chair, a cushion. And at home, create a touch sanctuary in your bed for better sleep: soft sheets, fluffy pillows, a warm plush comforter (unless you're menopausal like me). We don't have to stay in five-star hotels to have five-star sheets!

e. **Your nose:** This is the coolest sense!! The receptors in your nose have nerve endings that travel to two special places in your brain—the amygdala and the hippocampus. The amygdala is the part of your brain responsible for your emotions. The hippocampus controls consolidation of your memories. So, the scents go immediately to your emotion/memory centers. Your other senses do not work this way. Smell doesn't help you to remember things, but the things that you do remember will elicit more emotions.

So use that! Have smells in your classroom that take you to a happy place. Maybe you love the smell of pine/cinnamon/spice because it reminds you of the holidays. Use a candle, lotion, or essential oils all year long!

There you have it: five tips to help manage your anxiety. At the end of the day, it is important to believe you are making a decision each day to teach. And it takes a *lot* to make all of this worth it. You work hard. You put your whole self into your work. You spend your own money. You take time away from family and friends. There are other serving professions that could say the same. All of them have sacrifices for the love of the job.

It could also be you do this for the money (LOL), benefits, or time off. If that is what you are in it for, it could make it harder to continue through many years—not impossible though!

If you decide to stay and the reason is that it works so well with your family, you can still make a good career, but you have to make a greater effort to find joy. It is certainly easier if you're there because mostly you love these kids. I was missing that.

No one knew. I did a great job! I did interesting activities. I always brought in the latest technology. I smiled and was engaging and energetic! I treated the kids well. But deep down, I was doing these things for reasons no one knew: perfectionism and what others thought of me. That made my life as a teacher very difficult.

In 2003 I married my husband Tim and we blended eight children, ages nine through seventeen. I was with teenagers all day and teenagers all night. After a year of this, I knew it was time to go, and I knew what I wanted to do. Several years prior to this, I had gotten together with some other teachers in my building, and we created a mentoring program for new teachers. During the trainings I would share some of my story. One day, Glenda, a central office staffer, came to one of the mentor trainings I was conducting. She came up to me at the end and said, "Wow, you really have a way of sharing that story and helping these new teachers—thank you so much!" It was then I decided I would devote the rest of my career to teaching adults and helping them with anxiety, stress, and other life challenges.

Back to our original question: What if . . . instead of your anxiety controlling you, you controlled *it*? I believe in you! I admire you! I trust in your ability to make decisions in your life that make you healthier and wiser. I absolutely, positively know that Jeremiah 29:11 is meant for you, personally! Every. Single. Day!

"'For I know the plans I have for you,' declares the Lord, 'plans to prosper you and not to harm you, plans to give you hope and a future.'"

Use this scripture as well as the tips in this chapter to find rest for your soul!

Journal Prompt:

We all have anxiety from time to time, some more than others. Admit it. Don't be ashamed. Don't beat yourself up. Get help. Pray. Learn. Grow. And *please* try the tips, take control of anxiety, and find rest for your soul. As you do, keep the following two questions in mind:

1. Which action step will you implement in the next week to help curb your anxiety?

2. How do you think implementing this step will move you forward?

I pray that God blesses you, keeps you, and directs you, whether it be with students or some other fabulous path in your life!

Love & Hugs

10
A TIME FOR EMOTIONS

Dr. Tami West

**"... *a time to weep, and a time to laugh;*
a time to mourn, and a time to dance."**
Ecclesiastes 3:4

W HAT IF YOU WERE ABLE TO *experience* a range of emotions without *becoming* them?

> I remember it like it was yesterday: One minute we were staining onion skins to examine under the microscope. The next minute we were watching television screens as planes crashed into the Twin Towers in New York City.
>
> 9/11/2001

You likely have a memory like this if you were teaching on September 11, 2001. You might have a different memory, maybe as a mom, a student, or even a small child. Heck, I hate to think of how old I am getting, but at some point someone will read this who wasn't even born then!

That year I was team-teaching two out of my three classes of Honors Biology. We had about forty students in the biology lab, and they were excited (Oh wait, maybe *we* were the ones excited) about looking at the little purple cells. I remember us glancing at one another. *What do we do? Do we tell them? Do we stop class? Do we call people we know? Do we scream? Cry? Curl into little balls under the lab tables?*

As a teacher, you probably know what we did—we stuffed our emotions into that little teacher pocket, turned off the televisions, and continued looking at those magnificent purple blobs!

There is a second story in contrast to this one. I also remember it like it was yesterday. Same teacher. Same classroom.

This day I was teaching my class that wasn't co-taught (my *alone* class of the day) when my co-teacher walked in. Out of the corner of my eye, I saw her correcting one of my students. How do I even begin to relay to you what happened inside of me? Was I irritated? No. Was I angry? No. I was *enraged*!

Who does she think she is? This is not our class or her class! This is my class! Does she think I don't know how to manage my own classroom? How disrespectful! As with 9/11, I stuffed my feelings, put on a fake smile, and moved on. As the day went on and we interacted alone, she knew I was upset. I did the passive-aggressive thing:

"Are you mad?"

"No."

"Is something wrong?"

"No."

"Can we talk about it?"

"I told you—*there's nothing wrong!*"

I finally did tell her, and she cried. *Cried*!! *I made another teacher cry!*

I hope you don't think less of me for this, and I hope you will admit that you have felt/behaved this way before. If not, you probably don't need this chapter. Looking back, many years later, here is what I take away from these stories—the reason I share them with you:

My time teaching was post-mental hospital.

I had been through extensive counseling. I had turned to God for healing. I had worked on my low self-esteem, feelings of worthlessness, anger, despair, anxiety, and depression. As serious as it was, on the day of 9/11 I was able to do what is called *deep acting.* Although I was feeling one way on the inside and acting another on the outside, I could reconcile the feelings and the actions. I knew I was doing what was best for my students. It had nothing to do with me and my own worth.

When it came to the other teacher correcting my student? Different story. That day, I did a very bad job of what is called *surface acting*—I had zero sense of reconciliation of my inside feelings versus my outside acting. This situation was more about me and my sense of competency as a teacher. This was different.

And *that* is what I am going to help you with here, something called *emotional labor.*

Have you ever been in a meeting with a parent whose kid has given you all sorts of trouble? They make excuse upon excuse, and what you *want* to do is wag your finger and say, "Are you kidding me?!!" But what you probably *do* is smile, grit your teeth, and say something like, "Yes, Mr. and Mrs. Jones, Charlie certainly does have a lot of potential that we are all trying to uncover." That is called Emotional Labor—*the process of feeling one way while acting another.* It means you are suppressing your true emotions, which can be draining if you don't manage it.

The example I gave you with Charlie is one of *surface acting.* You probably don't buy anything the parents are saying. You might even doubt Charlie's true potential, and you don't feel one ounce of what is coming out of your face and your mouth! I want to help you move from surface acting to deep acting. Deep acting occurs when, yes, you are frustrated with Charlie, and yes, you don't love it when parents make what we think are excuses, but somewhere deep inside, you are able to reconcile what you are feeling with how you are acting.

Following are three tips to help you reconcile feelings with actions and have a more mature, more satisfying, less draining emotional life:

1. Understand the emotional part that is out of your control.

If I have heard it once, I have heard it a million times: "Well, I can't help it, I just get mad easily! I just can't help it I cry all the time! That's just how I am!" It's time to understand that is partly true and partly false. The theory of emotions that I subscribe to (Ekman, 1999)[1] is that we are all hard-wired with certain basic emotions. These emotions stay the same throughout your entire life unless disease or injury causes a change. You don't control them; they rear up before you have a chance to think. These emotions include joy, sadness, anger, and fear.

So why these? Why do we have these God-given emotions? Think about babies. These emotions serve specific functions and are hard-wired in all of us beginning early in life. Let's take, for example, the emotion joy. Babies start smiling within weeks of birth. When you see a baby smile, what do you do? You smile back. And what happens? You form a connection. It's the same thing throughout life. When you hear the words, "Your smile might be the only one someone sees all day," it's really true; use it wisely. A biological reaction allows humans to bond through smiling.

Let's look at one more emotion—anger—and then I think you will get the point. Honestly, you probably don't need help to manage the joy in your life! Anger and sadness are typically the two that you might like some help with. If you see a baby screaming and wailing, and you know that baby is angry, what do you do? You tend to look for something that is wrong. Diaper? Hungry? What is upsetting this little child? The same thing with adults. The basic emotion of anger exists to help you correct things that are wrong. There is more to it than this, and we will come to that in a minute. But the emotion of anger is not a bad thing.

What to do:

a. First, don't beat yourself up about your particular level of emotions. For example, maybe you anger easily or feel sad more often than most. Recognize that there is a genetic component to your emotions. Also, remember, as a woman, you also battle hormonal fluctuations that influence your emotions. Your emotional responses are real!

b. Second, don't judge everyone else's level of emotions by your standard. It is very easy, for example, for someone genetically wired to be happy all the time to expect everyone else to be that way as well. It is very easy for someone with a high level of anger to not understand why things don't bother other people. Using your own emotional level as the "correctness gauge" for everyone else is not only unfair to them, it is also very frustrating for you.

c. Don't use your level of emotions as an excuse. Staying with the example of anger, for instance, avoid saying things such as, *Well, I blow up easily! Everyone knows it. It's just how I'm wired!* As you are about to learn, emotions are not completely out of your control.

131

2. Understand the emotional part that is under your control.

The basic emotions we just covered reside deep in your brain stem. You might know that you also have another part of your brain called the *cerebrum*, the thinking part of your brain. Here is a story to describe the transition from lack of control to control. My husband sells hearing aids nationwide, so he travels every week (different hotel each week). Recently, he told me about a dream. He was in a meeting. (He hates meetings!) He decided to find a way out and saw a door close by. He opened the door and walked into the hallway. The light was so bright, it woke him up. He wasn't dreaming. He was walking in his sleep!! He was in the hallway of the Holiday Inn at 11:00 at night with nothing on but his tidy whities! No shirt. No pants. No shoes. No glasses. No key.

Imagine the basic emotion he felt when his eyes flew open—probably fear. But then what happened in his brain? *Oh, my gosh where am I? What am I going to do? What if someone sees me? What if there are children in the hall? What if they call the police? How can I get my key?* Suddenly, the basic emotion of fear morphed into the very complex emotion of terror or panic!

I don't want to leave you hanging—here is how the story ends, in my husband's own words: "I walked my thinly veiled behind to the elevator. I pressed "1" and the door opened near the desk. The clerk's mouth gaped open and I said 'I know. I was walking in my sleep. I need my key.' The clerk told me the key would get me in only once, which I said was all I needed. I got back in my room. Now I sleep in pants with pockets—and a key!"

Complex emotions have an element of control: how you think.

Of course we are going to have thoughts every second of every day, but most of those thoughts go unnoticed. For example, my husband didn't truly pay attention to most of the thoughts that increased his panic. People get upset in traffic. They pay no attention to the underlying thoughts and assumptions that lead to their rage.

Linda Elder and Richard Paul of The Foundation for Critical Thinking (criticalthinking.org) propose six stages in the development of mature thinking. Let's take a look at the first and the last stages to get a general idea of how thoughts can mature.

Per Elder and Paul, the first stage is called *the unreflective thinker*, which they describe as follows:

"Unreflective thinkers are largely unaware of the determining role that thinking is playing in their lives and of the many ways that problems in thinking are causing problems in their lives. Unreflective thinkers lack the ability to explicitly assess their thinking and improve it thereby."[2]

This person typically has an emotional episode but takes no time to assess where the emotion came from. Often they blame others for their anger, sadness, or fear.

The final stage is called *the accomplished thinker,* and they describe as follows:

"Accomplished thinkers not only have systematically taken charge of their thinking, but are also continually monitoring, revising, and re-thinking strategies for continual improvement of their thinking."[3]

Now *this* is where we want to be! I will be completely honest and say that some days I am spot-on and others, I am . . . well . . . you understand! This person has an emotional outburst and then takes time to analyze where the emotion came from. They self-assess. They actively analyze their thoughts.

What to do:

a. *Stop* each time you feel emotions welling up inside of you. Ask yourself what the emotion is, and pinpoint the thoughts you are having, just like I mentioned in my husband's sleepwalking story.

b. Become an Accomplished Thinker through practice. This means you regularly assess your thoughts. You try to find new solutions to problems. You do not assume the worst about each situation. I remember once being in a grocery store, trying to quickly buy some pita bread. I got to the section and another woman was already there looking through the selection. She looked and looked and looked. I felt my blood pressure elevate. I was shifting from foot to foot. So, I stopped. What was the emotion? Irritation! What was I thinking? *It's pita bread, how long can it take? Can't you see I'm standing here waiting? Do you not see me here?*

Funny thing is, a few seconds into this, the woman saw me and exclaimed, "Oh, I'm so sorry, I'm zoned out!" What did I say? "Oh, you're fine!" Episode over. If I had been practicing the Accomplished Thinking longer, I would have realized quickly this woman probably wasn't trying to ruin my day. Practice this with your students and coworkers as well.

Think of our earlier student, Charlie. Think of the assumptions you might make about your students and/or their parents that escalate your emotions. Some might be true; others are not. Often you don't even know you are having the thought.

3. Use language to temper emotions—yours and theirs.

Recall my co-teacher story from earlier when she reprimanded my student. Several times she asked me if I was mad, and I said *no*, even though I was livid. You have probably done this before, and we both know you were mad! My field of study rests here, with language. If I asked you to define what language is, you would probably say something like *a way to relay my thoughts; a window into my mind and heart.*

It's not that this is completely false. This assumption that language is a window into the mind indicates the presence of a private language that exists to communicate thoughts from one person to another. Words are meaningful only when others create their meanings. Therefore, words cannot be windows into simple thoughts. Not only are words not necessarily indicative of what you are thinking, words are actions—people do things with language.

Back to the *no* answer to the question "Are you mad?" Notice that, first, it certainly isn't indicative of what you are thinking. Second, you and I are doing something when we say it. It might be self-protection from an argument. It might be to keep the other person in turmoil. It might be to give ourselves more time to process. Maybe it's to create the appearance of maturity on your part. Lots of options!

Let's begin using language to our advantage.

What to do:

a. Expand your emotional vocabulary.

One sign of great emotional wisdom is to more accurately pinpoint the emotion you are feeling.

Examples of phrases to avoid:

- "This is the worst semester/group of students/parents ever!"

- "He/She makes me so mad!"

- "I am furious!" (Unless you truly are.)

Examples of phrases to use instead:

- "I have had an awful half-hour!"

- "I get so angry when he/she _____ ."

- "I am frustrated/concerned/anxious/angry."

I've created an extensive list of emotional terms to help you more accurately describe what emotions you are feeling. Go to https://www.tamiwest.com/free-downloads and look for "My Emotional Vocabulary."

    b. Use powerful, confident language with others.

One of the best skills I developed was to learn how to speak to others when my emotions were elevated. One of my favorite books that helped me learn what to say is called *PowerPhrases* (www.tamiwest.com/resources/powerphrases). Author Meryl Runion's mantra is:

"Say what you mean, mean what you say, and don't be mean when you say it."[4]

Remember, language is action. What do you want to accomplish when you speak to someone while you are emotional? As women, we receive mixed messages about speaking up. Speak up too much and you get called the B word. Speak up too little and be considered a doormat. On top of this, during your workday you must go from communicating as an authority figure with students to being on an equal level with other adults. The complexity of these interactions can be very challenging, but with the right tools, these confident conversations are doable and satisfying on so many levels! Think of how confident you could be with parents like Charlie's.

Here are a couple of examples of phrases to use when you are emotional:

- "I am angry because . . . "

- "I was embarrassed when you corrected my student while I was there."

- "I'm concerned when Charlie . . . "

An underlying reason for not using confident, non-aggressive language is that some people believe it makes them weak if they don't lash out. The effect is quite the opposite; powerful language makes you look and feel confident! The more you practice, the more emotional power you have.

These are tips that have made a difference in my life. How have I changed? Several years ago, Tim and I moved into a house on five acres in the woods. My father-in-law lives nearby, and I remember him saying to us, "Well, be prepared—it gets dark out here at night!" I thought, *Well, duh, it is dark everywhere at night!* We moved in and *then* I understood what he meant. There weren't a lot of streetlights and city lights to glow into our home, so it really was *dark!*

Tim and I are in our fifties, and so we get up a lot at night, you know—back and forth to the restroom. We would occasionally bump into each other. Stubbed our toes. Ran into walls. One night, our nightly ritual reached a whole new level of confusion. This is probably going to be way too much information, but here goes:

I was in the restroom, seated. You know how when you have to get up at night, you kind of try to keep your eyes squeezed shut as much as possible to keep from waking up? Well, my eyes were pretty squeezed, when I sensed a presence. I opened my eyes to see my husband, standing, in position with *his* eyes closed! I screamed. He screamed. A disaster was prevented. And . . . we bought a night light!

We laughed about how bad things had to get before we made a change—buying the light.

Shortly after, I was writing a presentation about change, and we laughed about this again. We were talking about the *old* me—the one who threw things and felt guilty and fearful.

The one who didn't want to live. The one who felt helpless and hopeless. Tim asked me a very simple but deep question that I want to ask you: "What made you decide to change?"

I had never thought of it that way before, but I guess that was what happened. The pain was so bad, I decided to change. Change wasn't easy. Change wasn't quick. Change is ongoing. The old me would scream and throw things. She made a teacher cry. She couldn't understand her students, coworkers, or parents. She would be irritated by traffic and shoppers, family and friends. She blamed her emotions on everyone and everything in her life.

The *new* me is still genetically wired with basic emotions and with levels of those basic emotions. I still get irritated and angry more easily than I would like to. I have to stop *often* to pinpoint my emotions and thoughts that escalate them. The difference now is, I *know* I'm more in control than I had ever been before. I don't have to live solely at the mercy of my biology. I can make better choices. You can, too.

I think back to those two stories I shared with you and the difference in this phenomenon we have discussed, Emotional Labor. It felt appropriate to put on a happy face for my students as the world was changing before my very eyes on 9/11. Of course, I felt fear, anger, and sadness, but my students needed a time of protection. I wasn't being asked to put on a mask for something I didn't believe in. My self-esteem was intact. My acting was deep.

The co-teaching experience was so different. It did *not* feel right to put on the happy face. My acting was shallow.

We have emotions for a reason. Don't hate them; instead, learn about them and use them. There are seasons to weep, to laugh, to mourn, and to dance; God told us there would be. But it is so worthwhile for me to trust in Him *and* change what needs to be changed. I know it will be for you, too!

Journal Prompt:

As you venture into your new emotional life, I ask you these three questions:

- Which emotion would you like to better manage?
- How will you begin working on that today?
- What would you like the *new you* to look like to you, your friends and family, colleagues, and your students?

May God bless you during each step of the way!

NOTES

Chapter 1 Clark Love

1.   Moran, Caitlin, *How to Be a Woman*. HarperCollins Publishers: New York, 2011.

Chapter 5 Severson

1.   Schawbel, Don, October 9, 2013, "Shawn Achor: What You Need to Do Before Experiencing Happiness," *Forbes*, November 21, 2017.

2.   Ekman, Paul, *Emotions Revealed: Recognizing Faces and Feeling to Improve Communication and Emotional Life*. Henry Holt: New York, 2007.

3.   Rodsky, Eve, *Fair Play: A Game-Changing Solution for When You Have Too Much to Do (and More Life to Live)*. G. P. Putnam's Sons: New York, 2019.

4.   Levin, T, *Calm*, Apple App Store version 1.2.0.2, 2018.

5.   Smith, Ora, "The Secret Life of the Brain," *Science*, Volume 295, No. 5553, 2002, p. 282.

Chapter 7 Smith

1.   Simmons, Michael, "I Spent Years Discovering the Simple Tactics Gurus Like Oprah, Einstein, and

Buffet Used to Become Successful—Here They Are."
QZ.com, August 17, 2017.

2. Tanner, Kimberly D., "Promoting Student Metacognition." *The American Society for Cell Biology,* Summer 2012, ncbi.nlm.nih.gov/pmc/articles/PMC3366894/(Promoting Student Metacognition).

3. *Reflective Impact Journal: Pursuing Greatness Every Day.* McRel International, Denver, Colorado.

Chapter 10 West

1. Ekman, P., "Basic Emotions." In T. Dalgleish's and M. Power's (Eds) *Handbook of Cognition and Emotion.* John Wiley & Sons, Ltd., Sussex, U.K., 1999.

2. Elder, Linda, and Richard Paul, The Foundation for Critical Thinking, criticalthinking.org.

3. Ibid.

4. Runion, Meryl, *PowerPhrases.* Power Potential Publishing: Cascade, Colorado, 2008, p. 19.

Made in the USA
Monee, IL
30 September 2020